# THE SOCIOLOGY OF EMOTIONS

Feminist, Cultural and Sociological Perspectives

Ann Brooks

First published in Great Britain in 2024 by

Bristol University Press
University of Bristol
1–9 Old Park Hill
Bristol
BS2 8BB
UK
t: +44 (0)117 374 6645
e: bup-info@bristol.ac.uk

Details of international sales and distribution partners are available at bristoluniversitypress.co.uk

© Bristol University Press 2024

British Library Cataloguing in Publication Data
A catalogue record for this book is available from the British Library

ISBN 978-1-5292-1732-2 hardcover
ISBN 978-1-5292-1733-9 paperback
ISBN 978-1-5292-1734-6 ePub
ISBN 978-1-5292-1735-3 ePdf

The right of Ann Brooks to be identified as author of this work has been asserted by her in accordance with the Copyright, Designs and Patents Act 1988.

All rights reserved: no part of this publication may be reproduced, stored in a retrieval system, or transmitted in any form or by any means, electronic, mechanical, photocopying, recording, or otherwise without the prior permission of Bristol University Press.

Every reasonable effort has been made to obtain permission to reproduce copyrighted material. If, however, anyone knows of an oversight, please contact the publisher.

The statements and opinions contained within this publication are solely those of the author and not of the University of Bristol or Bristol University Press. The University of Bristol and Bristol University Press disclaim responsibility for any injury to persons or property resulting from any material published in this publication.

Bristol University Press works to counter discrimination on grounds of gender, race, disability, age and sexuality.

Cover design: Andrew Corbett
Front cover image: Shutterstock/romi49
Bristol University Press uses environmentally responsible print partners.
Printed and bound in Great Britain by CPI Group (UK) Ltd, Croydon, CR0 4YY

# Contents

| | | |
|---|---|---|
| Notes on the Author | | iv |
| Acknowledgements | | v |
| Introduction | | 1 |
| 1 | The Language of Emotions: Concepts and Perspectives on the Emotions | 9 |
| 2 | The History of Emotions: The Emotions in Modernity | 20 |
| 3 | Privatized Emotions: Emotional Complexity in Late Modernity | 29 |
| 4 | Emotional Intersections: Gender in Emotions | 38 |
| 5 | Emotional Capital and Emotional Commodities | 53 |
| 6 | Positive and Negative Emotions | 67 |
| 7 | Emotions, Love and Intimacy | 78 |
| Bibliography | | 94 |
| Index | | 113 |

# Notes on the Author

Professor Ann Brooks was recently Research Fellow at the Institute of Advanced Studies in the Humanities at the University of Edinburgh. She is Fellow of the Academy of Social Sciences (FAcSS). Ann has held senior academic positions in Australia, Singapore, the UK and New Zealand. Ann has authored 14 books/monographs including *Academic Women* (Open University Press, 1997); *Postfeminisms: Feminism, Cultural Theory and Cultural Forms* (Routledge, 1997); *Gender and the Restructured University* (Open University Press, 2001); *Gendered Work in Asian Cities: the New Economy and Changing Labour Markets* (Ashgate, 2006); *Social Theory in Contemporary Asia* (Routledge, 2010); *Gender, Emotions and Labour Markets: Asian and Western Perspectives* (Routledge, 2011 and 2013) (with Theresa Devasayaham); *Emotions in Transmigration: Transformation, Movement and Identity* (Palgrave, 2014) (with Ruth Simpson); *Popular Culture, Global Intercultural Perspectives* (Palgrave, 2014); *Consumption, Rights and States: Comparing Singapore with Cities in Asia and the West* (Anthem, 2014) (with Lionel Wee); *Emotions and Social Change: Historical and Sociological Perspectives* (Routledge, 2014 and 2016) (co-edited with David Lemmings); *Genealogies of Emotions, Intimacy and Desire: Theories of Changes in Emotional Regimes from Medieval Society to Late Modernity* (Routledge New York, 2017); *Women, Politics and the Public Sphere* (Bristol University Press/Policy Press, 2019) and *Love and Intimacy in Contemporary Society: Love in an International Context* (Routledge, 2019/20). Ann's latest publication is an edited collection *The Routledge Companion to Romantic Love* (2022).

# Acknowledgements

I would like to acknowledge the support of a number of individuals and institutions in the production of this book. At the University of Edinburgh, my time as a Research Fellow at the Institute of Advanced Studies in the Humanities (IASH) provided a rich intellectual environment and research culture to undertake work on the book. I would particularly like to thank the Director of IASH, Ben Fletcher-Watson, for the support provided as well as the entire team at IASH. I also want to acknowledge the ongoing and invaluable support of Professors Catherine Roach and Theodore Trost, from the University of Alabama, who contributed significantly to the intellectual vitality of IASH as Research Fellows. At Bristol University Press (BUP), Victoria Pittman, Editorial Director at BUP, has provided outstanding editorial guidance throughout. My thanks to Anna Richardson, Senior Editorial Assistant at BUP, for maintaining editorial scrutiny throughout.

# Introduction

The analysis of the emotions is an interdisciplinary project and this book, *The Sociology of Emotions: Feminist, Cultural and Sociological Perspectives*, brings together a range of different perspectives in the process. These include feminist, cultural and sociological perspectives. Some describe the emotions as a 'subfield' of major disciplinary areas such as sociology and cultural studies. Others draw on the theorization and conceptualization of the emotions as developing and amplifying other disciplinary areas such as feminism.

Emotions have been the subject of extensive interdisciplinary analysis over the last 25 years, much of which has drawn on the intersection of sociology and the emotions, including Barbalet (2002, 2004), Shields (2002), Denzin (2007), Brooks (2014), Lemmings and Brooks (2014) and Jacobsen (2019). These are just a small number of the extensive range of publications in the field.

In this book the author focuses on an analysis of contemporary models and thinkers in the field. While there is an acknowledgement of classical thinkers and perspectives in the field, the focus is on more recent thinkers from across sociology, cultural theory and feminism. Many have made a significant contribution to the field of emotions and have produced an interdisciplinary and vibrant disciplinary field.

The book considers three dimensions in the analysis of emotions: the first considers conceptualizing emotions; the second considers theorizing emotions; and the third analyzing emotions.

- In conceptualizing emotions, the book explores the language of emotions looking at macro and micro framing of emotions, including: emotions in modernity and in late modernity; emotional labour; emotional capital and emotional commodities; positive and negative emotions; gender and emotions; masculinity and emotions; love, intimacy and emotions.
- The theorizing of emotions has been slow compared to other areas of theoretical development in sociology. However, both classical and

contemporary sociological theories show an understanding of emotions. This is captured across a range of social theories which will be covered throughout the book. Powell and Gilbert (2008: 394) note that the theorizing of emotions has been developing, but is still on the periphery of social theorizing (Layder, 2004, 2006). Both classical and contemporary social theorizing have indications of understanding the emotions theoretically and this includes for classical social theories – the rise of Enlightenment philosophy and additionally Kant's analysis of rationality (see Chapter 2).

This can be seen in classical social theory as follows: '… in Weber's concerns for legitimation, status, charisma, tradition and rationality; in Durkheim's theory of social solidarity, moral force and symbolism; in Marx on alienation, class consciousness and conflict mobilisation; … in G.H. Mead's and Goffman's theories of symbolic interactionism' (Powell and Gilbert, 2008: 394).

In relation to contemporary theorizing there is also important engagement with key thinkers, as Powell and Gilbert (2008: 395) also note in the engagement of key contemporary thinkers with the emotions. In the case of Giddens, the theorizing of 'ontological insecurity and risk'; in the case of Pierre Bourdieu, his focus on how individuals are exposed to 'life's daily emotional contingencies' and how they strive to cope. They also note that in feminist theorizing, emotions are shaped by patriarchy (Marshall and Witz, 2004). In relation to postmodernism, they show how emotions are becoming 'simulated in hyper-reality' (Baudrillard, 2005). Finally, they argue that the analysis of consumerism shows how desire and irrationality combine in conjunction with capitalism to shape individuality (Boden and Williams, 2002).

- Thirdly, the book focuses on an analysis of emotions which is wide-ranging and includes empirical and conceptual research on some of the key concepts. This includes both positive and negative emotions, happiness, anger, fear, love, friendship, sadness, depression, sympathy, shame and grief, among others.

Sociology has been slow to understand the significance of emotions as they impact on behaviour and everyday life. While there have been specific studies of 'happiness', or broad psycho-social collections of the analysis of emotions (Greco and Stenner, 2008), there has been a limited thoroughgoing analysis of how emotions contribute to sociology. The approach taken in this book is interdisciplinary, drawing on different branches of feminism, cultural theory, gender studies, politics and history and showing how the intersection of these different disciplinary areas provides an invaluable and original understanding of motivation, reflexivity and change. The interdisciplinarity of the approach is relevant for a more reflexive understanding of behaviour (see Burkitt, 1997, 2002, 2012; Brooks, 2008; Brooks and Wee, 2008; Cottingham, 2016; see also Chapter 2 of this book).

## Aims of the book

The specific aims of the book are as follows:

1. To bring together a wide range of approaches to and studies of emotions in the context of different substantive areas, including emotional complexity in late modernity; emotional labour; gender and sexuality; emotional capital and emotional commodities; positive and negative emotions; love and intimacy.
2. To provide an accessible, original and readable analysis of classical and contemporary cultural, feminist and sociological theories and studies which focus on emotions.
3. The book, while not a textbook, aims to provide a rich engagement with hundreds of studies and articles in the field, as can be seen from the bibliography, and thus provide an invaluable resource and source book for teaching in the sociology of emotions.

## Contents

*The Sociology of Emotions: Feminist, Cultural and Sociological Perspectives* brings together conceptual and theoretical analysis and a wide-ranging focus on studies of emotion. The book is an interdisciplinary analysis drawing on feminist, cultural and sociological perspectives. The book explores the 'language of emotion' looking at macro and micro framing of emotions, including: emotions in modernity; emotional labour and capital; public emotions; positive and negative emotions; masculinity and emotions; love, intimacy and emotions. The book studies both positive and negative emotions, including happiness, anger, fear, love, friendship, sadness, depression, sympathy, shame and grief, among others. The study of emotions is a relevant area of study for a more reflexive understanding of emotions.

## Introduction

The Introduction sets out the framework of the book which is organized around three dimensions: conceptualizing emotions, theorizing emotions and analyzing emotions. All the chapters address these dimensions, which are embedded within the substantive areas. A summary of these dimensions was outlined in the synopsis earlier. Stets (2012: 327) argues that 'while sociologists have been making theoretical advances on emotions, they have been moving beyond an analysis of positive and negative emotions to examine specific emotions.' This can include a wide range of emotions as outlined earlier. The breadth of emotions examined includes emotions such as happiness and anger and moral emotions such as guilt and shame.

## Chapter 1. The Language of Emotions: Concepts and Perspectives on the Emotions

Chapter 1 covers two major areas within the language of emotions, the first covers the conceptual framework of emotions and looks at how different emotions have gained contemporary currency. These include positive and negative emotions: happiness, anger, fear, love, friendship, sadness, depression, sympathy, shame and grief, among others.

Examples include studies of 'happiness', such as Yang's (2008) study. This is outlined more fully in Chapter 1. Yang found that differences in one's position in the social structure diminished with age. Yang's research also shows that women are happier than men and White people are happier than Black people and that those with a higher education are happier than those with a lower education. Yang found that the reduction in differences in happiness across sex, 'race' and education in conjunction with age could be due to people experiencing common life events which can offset differences. These could include the death of a spouse/partner or relatives and friends' declining health, as well as worries about social welfare benefits in an American context.

Another example is that of 'anger', as Schieman (2006) shows through an analysis of work, family and neighbourhood. This is outlined more fully in Chapter 1. Schieman shows that anger appears to be lower among older than younger individuals, thus indicating that anger diminishes over the life course. However, he shows that there are some gender differences in the expression of anger. He argues that while men and women do not differ in the frequency with which they experience anger, women are more likely to experience more intensive anger. He also maintains that once they are angered, men are more likely to use substances (see Schieman, 2006; Simon and Lively, 2010). In fact, Simon and Lively (2010) maintain that the more intense and persistent anger of women compared to men may contribute to higher rates of depression among women.

The second dimension of the chapter covers perspectives on emotions, including feminist, cultural and sociological perspectives. Ahall's (2018) work is a good example of the intersection of feminism and the emotions. In 'Affect as methodology: feminism and the politics of emotion', Ahall (2018) considers the political meaning of the 'affective-turn' in feminism. One of the key theorists in the field is Sara Ahmed (2014) and as she

(Ahmed, 2014: 208) explains: 'I turned to emotions as they help me to explain not only how we are affected in this way or that, by this or that, but also how these judgements then hold or become agreed as shared perceptions.' Ahall shows how feminism unpacks the politics of emotion and provides an understanding of how gender is characterized and framed in normative terms.

Cultural perspectives on emotions draw on Bourdieu's (1984) concept of cultural capital, but 'emotional capital' also emerges from Bourdieu's theory of social practice. Cottingham (2016: 451) describes emotional capital as a form of cultural capital which is specific to the emotions, which cuts across situations which individuals draw on in distinct fields. Cottingham states that she views emotional capital as 'neither, wholly gender-neutral nor exclusively feminine'.

Thoits (2004: 372) maintains that the concept of emotional capital offers 'promise for furthering emotion scholarship' by establishing connections between individual responses to emotions with 'macro-structural forces' which include 'social order, social inequality and social cohesion'. This is an important point in understanding research on emotions.

Finally, sociological perspectives on emotions have a strong tradition in defining and understanding emotions. Some of the theorists covered in this area include Barbalet's (2004) 'Emotion in social life and social theory'; Burkitt's (2012) 'Emotional reflexivity: feeling emotion and imagination in reflexive dialogues'; and Turner's (2005) 'Conceptualizing emotions sociologically', in Turner and Stets (2005), *The Sociology of Emotions*.

## Chapter 2. The History of Emotions: The Emotions in Modernity

This chapter looks at three aspects of how emotions have been theorized. The first is to review how emotions have been understood within classical sociological theories; the second is to consider the intervention around 'civilizing emotions' (Elias, 1978/82; Brooks, 2014; Lemmings and Brooks, 2014); thirdly, the chapter focuses on contemporary sociological analysis in late modernity, including Foucault (1965, 1977), Bourdieu (1984), Beck (1992), Giddens (1992) and Baudrillard (2005).

## Chapter 3. Privatized Emotions: Emotional Complexity in Late Modernity

This chapter builds on Chapter 2 and considers emotional complexity in late modernity. It considers relational complexity and examines the work of a wide range of theorists contributing to this field. It also looks at gender and emotional complexity and explores gender differences in responses to complex emotions. Finally, it examines loneliness in late modernity and shows how this has become a focused area of research within the analysis of emotions in late modernity.

## Chapter 4. Emotional Intersections: Gender in Emotions

Chapter 4 is the first of two chapters looking at emotional intersections; this chapter focuses on gender, which includes feminism. Feminism has engaged fully with emotions and as Ahall (2018: 41) shows: 'a feminist approach to the politics of emotion through gender is about how we become invested in social norms, it is about the affective investments in gender as a social norm.' Central to the feminist perspective is power, as Ahall (2018: 43) comments: 'from a feminist poststructuralist perspective, gender is analysed as a discursive power relation, a logic that informs and produces global politics (Butler, 2011; see also Shepherd, 2015).'

This chapter examines the work of feminist scholars, including Berlant (1993, 2009), Butler (1997, 2004), Ahmed (2004, 2010) and Hemmings (2005, 2011), who have contributed to 'affect studies'. As Gorton (2007: 334) comments: '… they all explore "the way feeling is negotiated in the public sphere and experienced through the body".'

This chapter also looks beyond feminist discourses around affect and considers a range of contemporary feminist theoretical perspectives (Rottenberg, 2014a; Banet-Weiser, 2015, 2018; Gill and Orgad, 2015, 2017; Gill, 2017; Gill and Kanai, 2018; Brooks, 2022) which challenge hegemonic Anglo–American feminist perspectives around affect.

A second dimension of the chapter is concerned with masculinities and emotions. De Boise and Hearn (2017: 780), in an article entitled 'Are men getting more emotional? Critical sociological perspectives on men, masculinities and emotions', have challenged the idea of '"emotional inexpressivity" in men'. This chapter will review and analyze a wide range of research on the relationship between masculinity and emotions. As de Boise and Hearn (2017: 780) comment: 'A growing body of … social research, *has* demonstrated that men not only have an active understanding of their emotional lives (see e.g. Galasinski, 2004) but in many cases appear to practice a "more emotional" form of masculinity (Forrest, 2010; Holmes, 2015; Roberts, 2013) than previously documented or assumed.'

By contrast this chapter also looks at the work of O'Neill (2015a, 2015b), who provides a fascinating analysis of Eric Anderson's (2009) concept of 'inclusive masculinity' in his book *Inclusive Masculinity: The Changing Nature of Masculinities*. O'Neill champions the work of more contemporary feminist theorists and provides an original and distinctive feminist analysis to masculinities.

## Chapter 5. Emotional Capital and Emotional Commodities

Chapter 5 looks at a broad range of emotional intersections with class, which has played an important part in understanding emotions. As shown in earlier chapters, the work of Pierre Bourdieu (1984) in *Distinction: A Social Critique of the Judgement of Taste* is crucial in understanding emotions. The importance of this perspective highlights the link of cultural capital and emotional capital. As Cottingham (2016: 451) comments: '… the concept of emotional capital holds promise for furthering emotion scholarship by linking individual resources and processes to macro-structural forces, including "social order, social inequality and social cohesion" (Thoits, 2004: 372)'.

While class is important in understanding emotions, it is also the intersection of gender and class in understanding emotions which is significant for debates in this chapter. Reay (2005), in 'Gendering Bourdieu's concept of capital: emotional capital, women and social class', focuses on this intersection.

This chapter also examines more contemporary cultural theoretical analysis, examining the intersection of emotions, consumption and commodities as developed in the work of Eva Illouz, who examines the intersection of feminism and cultural theory. Illouz's extensive body of work provides a comprehensive analysis of the field. The author has examined Illouz's contribution to sociological and cultural studies discourses elsewhere (see Brooks, 2017, 2019a).

Finally, this chapter looks at how this work has been built upon in the intersectional analysis of capitalism, neoliberalism and 'confidence culture', as developed in the work of a range of contemporary feminist theorists.

## Chapter 6. Positive and Negative Emotions

Chapter 6 examines the diverse field of positive and negative emotions and examines a range of theoretical perspectives and substantive areas in the field. The distinction between positive and negative emotions is linked to the much-discredited set of discourses of the 'psy-sciences' and the emergence of the 'mental health industry' of the latter part of the 20th and early 21st centuries. As has been noted by Hill et al (2019), the growth of 'psychology, psychiatry and to a lesser extent medicine' has created an entire vocabulary around 'emotion, desire, pathology and despair' which have been translated into a range of positive and negative emotions. This is explored more fully in Chapter 6.

This chapter explores a range of conceptual frameworks and theories on the emotions, from cultural studies, feminist and sociological perspectives. The chapter opens with a critical analysis of happiness studies which has been the focus for a number of theorists. The chapter explores the reason for the emergence of happiness studies, which has formed an important set of interdisciplinary studies and theoretical perspectives in the field.

One of the early theorists who has investigated a range of positive and negative emotions including happiness, anger and wretchedness is Sara Ahmed (2004, 2010). In particular, Ahmed (2010) in *The Promise of Happiness* shows how emotion is central within the social and political framework of understanding.

The second part of the chapter looks at a number of other concepts, including anger and shame, drawing on the work of theorists including Henderson (2008) and Probyn (2004). The third part of the chapter examines how emotions intersect with issues of politics and war, which includes exploring the issue of individual and collective trauma as outlined in the work of the Jeffrey Alexander (2012). Finally, this chapter explores the issue of social abjection by drawing on the work of Imogen Tyler (2013) from her book *Revolting Subjects: Social Abjection and Resistance in Neoliberal Britain*, which examines the issue of social abjection and how it relates to broader issues of social justice.

## Chapter 7. Emotions, Love and Intimacy

Chapter 7 reviews the relationship of emotions, love and intimacy and looks at some of the key contributors to this growing field which includes contemporary theories of love and emotion. The chapter adopts a socio-historical perspective in analyzing the work of writers and theorists in the field, including Giddens (1991, 1992); Beck and Beck-Gernsheim ([1995] 2002); Illouz (1997a, 1997b, 1998, 2010, 2012); Shumway (2003); Gross (2005) and O'Neill (2015a, 2015b), as well as the author's earlier work in the field, Brooks (2017, 2019a). The chapter focuses on a wide range of earlier and contemporary theorists in the field and examines how they explore the issues of love and intimacy. The chapter is divided into three sections as follows: Part I. Romantic love and the emergence of intimacy; Part II. Romance as a postmodern condition: Illouz, love and the cultural contradictions of capitalism; Part III. 'Mediated intimacy' in heterosexual men.

The book draws on a wide range of interdisciplinary theories and concepts which cover classical and contemporary debates in the field of emotions. It also draws on a huge range of international theorists and research to highlight the vast array of work in the field. The book develops historical perspectives on how different thematic areas have evolved and focuses on lucid and succinct summaries of key debates and thinkers in the field.

# 1

# The Language of Emotions: Concepts and Perspectives on the Emotions

## Introduction

Chapter 1 covers two major areas within the language of emotions: the first covers the conceptual framework of emotions and looks at how different emotions have gained contemporary currency. These include both positive and negative emotions: happiness, anger, fear, love, friendship, sadness, depression, sympathy, shame and grief among others.

The second part of the chapter covers perspectives on emotions, including feminist, cultural and sociological perspectives. In 'Affect as methodology: feminism and the politics of emotion', Ahall (2018) considers the political meaning of the 'affective-turn' in feminism. One of the key feminist theorists in this field is Sara Ahmed (2014), as she (Ahmed, 2014: 208) explains: 'I turned to emotions as they help me to explain not only how we are affected in this way or that, by this or that, but also how these judgements then hold or become agreed as shared perceptions'. This chapter explores early feminist perspectives on emotions and highlights their importance for the intersection of feminism and emotions.

Cultural perspectives on emotions have been championed by the work of Eva Illouz (2007, 2008, 2014, 2018) among others. Illouz's work has more recently focused on the intersection of emotions, neoliberal capitalism and consumption, and the range of her work is explored for an understanding of cultural perspectives on the emotions. Illouz's work has encapsulated some of the most significant changes in cultural perspectives on emotions. The author charts these changes over the course of the book and considers the contribution of this significant theorist to debates in the field.

Finally, sociological perspectives on emotions have a strong tradition in defining and understanding emotions. Some of the theorists covered in this area include, among others: Hochschild (1979, 1983); Scheff (1990);

Barbalet (2002, 2004, 2009); Burkitt (2002); Turner (2009); Bericat (2016). The chapter considers some of the main trends in the sociology of emotions established by these theorists. It also considers shifts in the perspectives and the intersection with other theorists and traditions (Holmes, 2004; Wharton, 2009; Goodwin et al, 2014; among others).

## Part I. The language of emotions – concepts

A number of sociologists have attempted to group concepts around the emotions within a typology, although the exact significance of such typologies is unclear. Bericat (2016) offers a simple typology of primary and secondary emotions. Bericat (2016: 492) defines these categories as follows: 'Primary emotions are considered to be universal, physiological, of evolutionary relevance and biologically and neurologically innate, while secondary emotions, which can be a result of a combination of primary emotions, are socially and culturally conditioned.' Bericat goes on to say that according to 'Kemper (1978), the primary emotions are fear, anger, depression and satisfaction-happiness, aversion-fear, assertion-anger, disappointment-sadness, and startlement-surprise. Emotions such as guilt, shame, love, resentment, disappointment, and nostalgia are considered to be secondary emotions' (Bericat, 2016: 492).

So, to give more meaning to these frameworks, let's examine some of these concepts. Bericat focuses on two concepts, 'fear' and 'anger', and frames these as 'families of feelings'. For example, Bericat (2016) argues that 'fear' can be seen to cover a broad range of feelings, encompassing worry, anxiety, panic, terror or horror, which can be seen to differ both in content and in intensity of feeling. He draws on Barbalet's (2004) understanding of fear, which he describes as when future interests of actors are threatened. Barbalet also distinguishes between the cause of fear, which he identifies as vulnerability, and the wider context of the actor's relative lack of power in relation to a global event, which could be the object of fear which emerges from the prospect of suffering harm.

Another example provided by Bericat (2016) is that of 'anger', which again is shown as extending over an extensive range of emotions from simple annoyance or indignation to rage and fury. Bericat draws on Schieman (2006) in arguing that it often emerges by perceived or real injustice or insult or lack of equality, or barriers to achievement. Barbalet analyzes anger within the context of class (to be discussed later).

Stets (2012) is another theorist who provides an analysis of the concept of 'anger' and draws on ideas from a number of other theorists in the process. For example, Schieman (2006) provides three different contexts in which anger can emerge, including work, family and neighbourhood. In the context of work, a situation which provokes anger is perceived as inequality in the workplace. In the family, one of the main causes of anger is money. Other theorists, Lively and Powell (2006), made a comparison between anger emerging from the home and from work. They found that when anger emerged from the family, they were more likely to speak directly to family members, whereas in a work situation, where anger emerges they are more likely to approach the issue in an indirect way by talking to others. This would seem to be obvious as a work situation provides a large number of bodies such as HR for defusing a situation and for mediation. Lively and Powell (2006) also found that unlike those angered at home, those angered at work were less likely to discuss it with others.

Stets shows that sociologists have been studying whether some social groups are more likely to express anger than others. Schieman (2006) maintains that anger appears to be lower among older individuals than younger individuals, thus anger declines over the life course. In addition, Stets (2012: 330) shows that there are some gender differences in the expression of anger. Women and men show differences in the frequency with which they experience anger; for example, women experience more intense anger than men, and are more likely to talk about their anger, whereas it is claimed that men are more likely to use substances (Schieman, 2006; Simon and Lively, 2010). Simon and Lively (2010) also go further and argue that the more intense and persistent anger of women compared to men could be a contributing factor to women's high rates of depression.

One of the contributing factors in the expression of anger outlined by Collett and Lizardo (2010) is status. They studied two competing lines of research on status and anger; in the first, they found that those with low status are more likely to experience anger, as a result of discrimination and disadvantage. In the second line, 'high status people are more likely to experience anger, particularly in interactions with low status others, in which low-status others fail to defer or confirm the position of high-status persons' (Stets, 2012: 330). As might be expected, Collett and Lizardo found that low-status individuals expressed anger as a result of a lack of control over their situation, whereas high-status individuals tend to direct their anger at low-status individuals.

Another major concept identified by Stets is that of happiness, which reflects the interests of a number of theorists (Schnittker, 2008; Yang, 2008; Ahmed, 2010) (see also Chapter 6). Stets (2012) draws on two interesting studies of national data on happiness, both from the US, which examine trends in happiness over a 30-year period, starting in 1972. These are studies by Schnittker (2008) and Yang (2008). In Schnittker's study, his analysis revealed that happiness has increased in the US over a 30-year period (1973–2004). Schnittker found that this increase was associated with two factors, the first a rise in income and the second a growing participation in the labour force.

Another study by Yang (2008) provides additional insights over the 30-year period by providing more granular detail around age, period and cohort effects. Yang showed that on the issue of age, as one gets older, happiness increases. He found that maturity is partially responsible and that in addition he found that disparities in happiness based on one's position in the social structure diminished with age.

Research in the US also shows that women are happier than men, White people are happier than Black people, and those with higher education are happier than those with less education.

> Yang argued that the reduction in differences in happiness across sex, race, and education with age may be due to individuals experiencing common life events that help equalize differences such as on the one hand, the death of a spouse/partner, relatives and friends, declining health, and on the other social welfare benefits. (Stets, 2012: 329)

Yang did refine the results further, showing higher levels of happiness over some periods than others. For example, happiness rose from the mid-1990s until 2004. In addition, baby boomers were found to be less happy than earlier or more recent cohorts, which Yang maintains could be the result of greater competition in the educational system and labour market.

A further concept relevant to this area is 'shame'. As Ahmed (2004) points out, shame comes from the self-realization of one's own deficiency. It is different from guilt; a sense of guilty feelings involves doing something wrong and can be compensated in the future. Shame, argues Ahmed, is self-evaluation and imagined evaluation from others. Shame is a relationship between self and others. Shame is not an inner quality, possessed by self; rather, shame exists in the interaction between self and the other and self's evaluation of such interaction. Sedgwick (2003) interprets shame as the attempt to reconstruct human interaction. She thinks shame is the place where the question of identity arises most originally and relationally (Sedgwick, 2003: 36–37). We should be aware that Sedgwick does not mean that identity originates from a sense of shame, rather she emphasizes that identity manifests as a question or a crisis, and the sense of shame is the place where identity questions emerge in relationship to others.

## Part II. Perspectives on the emotions

The second part of the chapter focuses on different perspectives on the emotions, drawing on sociological, cultural and feminist perspectives.

### Sociological perspectives on the emotions

The intersection of sociology and the emotions provides a rich body of historical, theoretical and substantive research which continues to evolve.

The range of the interaction of sociology and emotions is enormous and a large part of the sociological research from the US is influenced by psychological research, which undermines mainstream sociological research which focuses on the social nature of human relations (Burkitt, 2002; Bericat, 2005, 2016; Barbalet, 2009). Thus, while the analysis here draws on theorists from the US, there is an emphasis on the sociological definition of emotions. Barbalet (2004: 8–9) maintains that 'sociology has something to say about the emotions for two reasons: first because sociology seeks to explain social phenomena, and emotion is a social phenomenon; and second because emotion is necessary to explain the fundamentals of social behaviour.' Elsewhere, Bericat (2000) asserts a sociological explanation is incomplete if it fails to include an understanding of emotions in the form of incorporating the 'feeling subject' into an understanding of social structures and social processes.

Many theorists and analysts note that the sociology of emotions as a subfield started developing in the 1970s, but in fact there were elements of the emotions within classical sociological theories during sociology's first century. Turner (2009) succinctly comments that Karl Marx was concerned with alienation, which has emotions at its core, as well as the suffering and deprivation of the proletariat which is suffused with emotion. In the case of Max Weber, his view of types of action includes 'affect', whereas George Simmel's focus on conflict emphasizes 'emotional arousal' as part of the process of the mobilization of conflict. Another classical theorist, Émile Durkheim, in his analysis of the origins of religion, focuses on the concept of 'effervescence' as an emotional aspect of his theory of social solidarity. Finally, Vilfredo Pareto articulates views on 'sentiments' and 'deprivations' which shows an emotional underpinning for 'the cyclical dynamics of societies', a central element of his theory.

Bericat contextualizes the historical debates and shows that 20th-century sociology virtually ignored the study of emotions in both social theory and research as a result of 'the hegemony ultimately reached by cognitivism' (2016: 497). It was only in the 1970s that debates around the emotions in sociology began to open up around the research of three theorists: Arlie Hochschild, Thomas Scheff and Theodore Kemper. Hochschild (1979, 1983) drew on Goffman's early work by conceptualizing 'an emotion culture', and Bericat (2000) states that Hochschild was the first to use the phrase 'the sociology of emotions' in 1975. In 1979 Hochschild published an article in which she introduced concepts such as 'feeling rules' and 'emotion work' and her work shows how culture defines what, when and how we should feel.

One of the foremost sociologists who contributed to the analysis of emotions is Arlie Hochschild. Her work combines theoretical sophistication and feminist underpinnings with real life application. Hochschild's book (1983) *The Managed Heart: The Commercialization of Human Feeling* was ground breaking and showed how service workers engaged in emotion management, and she drew on flight attendants as an example. Hochschild's work is drawn on across this book to develop different aspects of her work for the sociology of emotions, including the intersection of gender and emotion, and for the development of the concepts of emotional labour and emotion work.

Thomas Scheff (1966, 1974, 2012) was a social interactionist and developed the idea of labelling theory in relation to mental illness. While he is regarded as a sociologist, his work interacts with social psychology and psychiatry, but his analysis is rooted in the thinking of sociologists such as Cooley, Goffman and Elias. Scheff's (2012: 1) 'A social/emotional theory of "mental illness"' maintains that one reason that theories of mental illness have made little progress is because they have focused on individuals, 'omitting the social/relational and emotional world'. Scheff in this article focuses on the emotion of shame, and states that: 'It is proposed that most symptoms of mental illness are products of shame and relational feedback loops: emotion and alienation can both spiral leading to further alienation and chaotic or hidden emotions'(Scheff, 2012: 1).

Thomas Scheff's work started to emerge in the 1970s and he developed his analysis in 1988 in his sociological theory of shame and pride (see Bericat, 2016). Scheff argues that shame and pride are fundamental social emotions and Bericat (2016: 502) states that 'Scheff's theory of shame is based on the assumption of "the maintenance of bonds as the most crucial human motive" (Scheff, 1990: 4)'.

Other theorists combine different areas of sociology with emotions. For example, Kemper (1978) was one of the earliest theorists to develop a theory of how emotions are influenced by power and status. Bericat (2016) also shows that social scientists have contributed to an understanding of a range of concepts related to emotions. These include: 'confidence and trust (Barbalet, 2004, 2009), empathy and sympathy (Clark, 1987), grief and sadness (Charmaz and Milligan, 2006; Jacoby, 2012), boredom (Barbalet, 1999), love (Illouz, 2012), horror (Bericat, 2005) and disgust (Douglas, 2002; Nussbaum, 2006)' (Bericat, 2016: 503). This is interesting and wide-ranging in identifying the scope of the emotions across a range of sociological theorists.

Stratification is another area of theory that impacts on emotions, as emotions are distributed across social classes. Barbalet's (2004) analysis of the intersection of social class and emotions is important. Barbalet's work is a significant contribution to a sociological analysis of the emotions and shows how power is a central feature in the analysis of social class and emotions.

Barbalet (2004) has maintained that a range of emotions including confidence, resentment, shame, vengefulness and fear are differentially distributed across social classes. For example, he draws on the emotion of fear, which he maintains occurs when members of a class lack power to pursue their interests. The model that Barbalet (2004) draws on covers a range of emotions including confidence, resentment, shame, vengefulness as well as fear and he maintains they are differentially distributed across different populations that hold different levels of power and prestige.

Turner (2009) makes the point that Barbalet's analysis is not wholly about negative emotions. Barbalet's focus on confidence shows that individuals feel confident when their future is predictable and under their control and he argues that as it is members of the more affluent and powerful classes who are most likely to be in control of their future, confidence tends to apply disproportionately to these classes.

## *The emotions in sociology*

The study of the emotions in sociology has been particularly vibrant in a number of fields including gender (Chapter 4), class and consumption (Chapter 5), love and intimacy (Chapter 7) and in areas of positive and negative emotions (Chapter 6). These areas are explored in the chapters of this book along with more nuanced areas.

The intersection of gender and the emotions has resulted in a wide range of theoretical and substantive areas and has in addition fed into other areas such as consumption (Chapter 5), intimacy (Chapter 7) and gender and work (Chapter 4). These fields and subfields are explored in these chapters.

## *Cultural theory and emotions*

The definition of cultural theory is very variable and cultural theory as understood through scholarship in the UK differs from the US and elsewhere. Illouz et al (2014: 222) define the role of emotions within cultural studies as follows: 'Emotions are at the interface of the individual's experience, collective meanings and social constraints (through such social emotions as shame, depression or anger). To say this differently: emotions are shaped by cultural models of the self, moral codes and forms of sociality.'

Illouz et al observe that a more sophisticated approach to the relationship between cultural standards regulating emotion and social structure can be found in the early work of Norbert Elias (1978) (see also Brooks, 2014; Lemmings and Brooks, 2014). Illouz et al outline his work as follows:

> In his classic work *The Civilizing Process*, Norbert Elias (1978) explores the development of nonviolent social interactions in the West from the twelfth century onward. The refinement of behaviour and affective reactions was the result of a long socio-historical process in Western societies by which human beings were drawn into ever-denser relations of mutual interdependence. (Illouz et al, 2014: 224)

In *The Civilizing Process*, Elias explores a variety of etiquette manuals from the 16th and 17th centuries and draws on them to identify a process by which standards were applied to a range of behaviours, including 'violence, sexual behaviour, emotional expression, bodily functions, eating habits, table manners and forms of speech' (Illouz et al, 2014: 224). These behaviours became increasingly self-policed and monitored by patterns of social etiquette and 'increased what we may call the threshold of shame, embarrassment and repugnance'(Illouz et al, 2014: 224). In other words, Elias charts the development of social mores and norms as society became increasingly sophisticated.

Contextualizing Elias's work, Illouz et al (2014: 225) show how Elias's work has contributed to the sociology of emotions more broadly. Elias's work *The Civilizing Process* did not set out to develop a sociology of emotions, but a wide range of sociological theorists (and others) have drawn on and elaborated the impact of his work for the history of emotions. These include Stearns and Lewis (1998), Reddy (2001) and Wouters (2007). It is argued by Illouz et al (2014: 225) that 'the most interesting line of inquiry is the one that has focused on emotional habitus (Burkitt, 1997: 43; Calhoun, 2001; Kane, 2001; Illouz, 2007, 2008).'

Central to much of Illouz's work (2007, 2008, 2018) is the 'emotional economy' (see also Chapter 5, Chapter 7) and she relates this to Elias's work. As Illouz et al (2014: 225) note: 'Elias's object of study is the system of emotional economy and its relation to social and political structures.' Illouz (2007, 2008) is particularly interested in the work of Norbert Elias because it surfaces explanations for the emergence of normative systems as well as patterns of emotional control in the capitalist workplace, which Elias identifies as the result of the intensification of social interactions and networks (see also Brooks, 2014; Lemmings and Brooks, 2014).

Elsewhere, Illouz (2018: 5) argues that 'far from heralding a loss of emotionality, capitalist culture has on the contrary been accompanied with an unprecedented intensification of emotional life with actors self-consciously pursuing and shaping emotional experiences for their own sake (Hochschild, 1983; Hardt and Negri, 2006; Illouz, 2007; Ahmed, 2010) …'. The intersection of emotions, capitalism, consumption and authenticity has occupied a lot of Illouz's more recent work and aspects of her work are examined in later chapters (see Chapter 5 and Chapter 7).

## Feminist perspectives on emotions
### Understanding emotions and affect. What is the 'affective turn'?

The intersection of feminism and the emotions is explored comprehensively in Chapters 4 and 5, which examine historical as well as contemporary models of feminism's engagement with the emotions. To avoid repetition, areas such as the feminist critique of the distinction between emotions and rationality (body–mind dichotomy) and subjective–objective distinctions which link women with one side of the distinction are fully explored in Chapters 4 and 5.

One of the key shifts in thinking from traditional models to contemporary models of feminist theorizing has been what is defined as the 'affective turn'. It provides a dividing line between traditional second-wave feminist thinking around concepts such as patriarchy to more contemporary thinking, critical of the hegemonic while Western model of feminist patriarchy to a more contemporary focus on consumption and neoliberalism as key aspects of a postfeminist perspective.

The impact of the 'affective turn' in the social sciences has also had broader theoretical implications in the transformation of ways of thinking about the self, identity and reflexivity. Feminism has of course been central in these debates (Brooks, 2008; Brooks and Wee, 2008; Pedwell and Whitehead, 2012; Ahall, 2018). Pedwell and Whitehead (2012: 115) are veteran commentators on the relationship between feminism and 'the affective turn' and they acknowledge that 'while "the affective turn" has gained significant currency over the last decade, it is nonetheless difficult to define as it has come to signify a range of different, and sometimes contradictory movements and articulations.'

Ahall (2018: 39) distinguishes between emotion and affect and argues that while emotion is understood 'as capturing conscious thought, subjective experiences and normative judgements belonging to the individual, affect refers to a completely different order of activity ... [and] can be understood as a set of embodied practices.' The author explores the relationship between feminism and affect as part of the historical evolution of feminism's intersection with the emotions in Chapter 4. Pedwell and Whitehead observe that:

> Feminist scholars have been at the heart of these engagements with affect, in part, because, for some, feminism is a politics 'suffused with feelings, passions and emotions' (Gorton, 2007: 333) but also one that has long recognised the critical links between affect and gendered, sexualized, racialised and class relations of power. (Pedwell and Whitehead, 2012: 116)

Ahall puts the emphasis on feminist scholars' critique of affect. She argues that:

> These feminist scholars have pointed out that any 'turn to affect' that privileges affect over emotion as its object for analysis, implies that there is something 'new' going on, when in fact, feminist theorists have long been concerned with the relationship between affect, knowledge and power (Pedwell and Whitehead, 2012: 119). (Ahall, 2018: 39)

Importantly, as Ahall (2018: 41) comments: 'a feminist approach to the politics of emotion through gender is about how we become invested in social norms, it is about the affective investments in gender as a social norm.' By this, as Ahall shows, feminism unpacks the politics of emotion and provides an understanding of how gender is characterized and framed in normative terms.

Central to the debate about feminism and affect is to what extent knowledge can be understood as objective. Feminist theory challenges the idea of knowledge as objective and, as Ahall (2018: 41) shows, 'focus on the importance of *being as a mode of knowing*'. Ahall also argues that in considering feminist knowledge on affect, she agrees with Pedwell and Whitehead (2012) who claim that feminist theory could achieve more by focusing on how affect offers possibilities for 'thinking (and feeling) beyond what is already known and assumed' (Pedwell and Whitehead, 2012: 117), rather than focusing on how affect may 'dominate, regulate and constrain individuals'.

Another 'big beast' of the 'affect' era is Sara Ahmed (2014), who compares the separation between affect and emotions to an egg: 'That we can separate them does not mean they are separate' (Ahmed, 2014: 210). Ahmed 'challenges the distinction between affect and emotions by discussing emotions as the idea of "impression", precisely to avoid making analytical distinctions between bodily sensation, emotion, and thought' (Ahall, 2018: 43).

A further discussion of the relationship between emotion and affect within feminist theory is developed in Chapter 4.

### The shift from 'affect' to 'consumption'

Contemporary feminism has moved on in its focus on emotions away from 'affect' to 'consumption'. A full analysis of this shift is given in Chapters 4 and 5. However, it is important to record the shift in feminism on these issues. In fact, it also reflects a shift in feminist theoretical thinking more generally towards a postfeminist analysis (see Chapters 4 and 5). We can argue that 'the affective turn' and its theorists was in large part 'a second wave' feminist development, whereas the current focus on feminism and consumption is a reflection of the postfeminist era (Illouz, 2009, 2018; Gill, 2017; Brooks, 2022).

This is an exciting, accessible approach to emotions, appealing to a new generation of feminists and focusing on the emotions within neoliberal capitalism and considering the emotions as a commodity (Illouz, 2018). As Illouz comments: 'Consumer capitalism has increasingly transformed emotions into commodities and it is this historical process which explains the intensification of emotional life' (Illouz, 2018: 10). Thus, most contemporary feminists make important theoretical links between emotions and capitalism and focus on the intensification of emotional life within capitalism. As noted by Illouz (2018: 5): 'Even casual observers can take note of the fact that in the second half of the twentieth century, personal life and emotional fulfilment have become central pursuits and preoccupations of the self'. Chapters 4 and 5 provide a comprehensive analysis of contemporary feminism and its relationship to the emotions within 'Western' capitalism.

## In summary

Chapter 1 has focused on two main areas in understanding the emotions; the first was the language of emotions, which covered the conceptual field surrounding the emotions and examined some of the major concepts. The second part of the chapter examined perspectives on the emotions and set out some of the major areas covering these fields. The three major perspectives examined in this chapter and throughout this book include: sociological perspectives on the emotions; cultural perspectives on the emotions; and feminist perspectives on the emotions.

2

# The History of Emotions: The Emotions in Modernity

## Introduction

The history of emotions in sociology draws on a range of socio-historical and theoretical dimensions which include a broad spectrum of classical and contemporary theorists. This chapter looks at four aspects of how emotions have been theorized in sociology. The first is to review how emotions have been understood within classical sociological theories; the second is to consider the intervention around 'civilizing emotions' (Elias, 1978/82; see also Brooks, 2014; Lemmings and Brooks, 2014); thirdly, the chapter focuses on contemporary sociological analysis in late modernity, including Foucault (1965, 1977), Bourdieu (1984), Beck (1992), Giddens (1992) and Baudrillard (2005). This last section will also focus on the 'emotionalization of reflexivity' and will lead into the broader debates around emotions in late modernity in Chapter 3.

## Part I. The emotions in classical sociological theories

Despite the lack of an explicit acknowledgement of the emotions in sociological theorizing, particularly in classical sociological theorizing, Powell and Gilbert (2008: 394) state: 'There are strong intimations of theoretical understanding of emotions in classical and contemporary social theories in the rise of Enlightenment philosophy and the consequences for emotion with Kant's analysis of rationality (Ritzer, 2004)'.

As the author has noted elsewhere (Brooks, 2014), when classical sociologists began offering models of modern society, they described modernity as a move away from the alleged emotionality of 'traditional societies'. Max Weber (1864–1920) described the spread of a bureaucratic form of rationality linked with capitalism, and Norbert Elias (1897–1990) wrote about the encroachment of a 'civilizing process' which included forms of effective restraint and self-control. As Brooks (2014) also notes:

> The binary between emotion and cognition has a long history in the social sciences and stretches back to conceptions of 'Enlightenment modernity' and of modern scientific knowledge. In fact, when emotion was directly addressed by the early social scientists 'it was typically associated with the primitive and embodied female' (Greco and Stenner, 2008: 5). Some of the theorists of emotion and 'affect' reflect two major strands around the self and social structures, for example: 'Elias wrote of the gradual encroachments of a "civilizing process" entailing ever increasing forms of affective restraint and disciplined self-control … Parsons … wrote of a trend towards "affective neutrality" as society differentiates itself into functional sub-systems'. (Brooks, 2014: 9)

Powell and Gilbert (2008) also note that the classical sociological theorists were fundamentally concerned with the idea of controlling unstable and irrational emotions and all offered different mechanisms or models for achieving this. At the core of these theories is the emphasis on rationality and the focus on science and scientific reasoning as being critical to control nature. For example, in the models drawn on by Max Weber and his emphasis on legitimation, status, charisma, tradition and nationality. In Émile Durkheim's analysis, his powerful theory of social solidarity and moral force. In Karl Marx's theory of alienation, class consciousness and class conflict. In Sigmund Freud's work on the mind and civilization. In G.H. Mead's and Goffman's theory of symbolic interactionism in taking on the role of the 'other'.

Key to debates in both classical and contemporary theorizing is the issue of rationality. Powell and Gilbert look at the intersection of structure, rationality and gender. He draws on the examples of Durkheim and Marx and shows that emotions, while not explicit in their work, were important dimensions in their thinking. Powell and Gilbert (2008: 397) show that in the case of Durkheim (1964), his work on social rituals showed that the representation of rituals in sacred objects provided the mechanisms that hold society together by establishing moral constraints. Powell and Gilbert maintain that the inherent emotionality of the rituals of interaction provide the 'glue' that keeps society together and religion is central in this.

In the case of Marx, Powell and Gilbert argue that in preventing alienation, which Marx advocates, an 'emotional consciousness' is produced which can be activated against capitalism. They also state that for both Durkheim and Marx, 'the problem of modernity was a recognition of alienation and normlessness that impinges on the regulation of individual behaviour' (Powell and Gilbert, 2008: 397).

*Emotion, rationality and gender*

Classical sociological theory has been overwhelmingly dominated by male theorists. Seidler (1994: ix-x) has traced the masculinity of social theory to the emphasis of reason over emotion within Enlightenment modernity. Seidler makes the point that central to an Enlightenment view of modernity is reason, and as the relationship of masculinity to modernity is critical, masculinity's identification with reason becomes the predominate one for Enlightenment modernity.

This theme is fairly consistent throughout both the classical and some later sociological theorists. This is not to argue that classical sociological theorists ignored the role of emotions and 'affect' entirely. Auguste Comte recognized the importance of the 'affective' over the 'intellectual' and understood that the 'affective faculties' were essential for the improvement of society (Lenzer, 1983). In fact, Comte understood the need for the 'affective faculties' to balance abstract reasoning. Comte saw 'sexual love' as a positive influence on society, but only when it was disciplined (Lenzer, 1983: 377). He saw marriage as providing that positive, and he went further in stating that divorce could not be considered and that the 'perpetuity of widowhood' was a 'moral duty' (Lenzer, 1983: 378; cited in Sydie, 2004: 39). Most of the classical theorists, including Durkheim, saw dysfunctionality arising in society when individualistic and sexual desires were not controlled.

## Part II. Contemporary social theory and the 'affective turn'

The work of Norbert Elias (1978/82) has provided an important source of ideas around the emotions drawn on by a number of theorists. As noted earlier, Elias's work has been important in understanding issues of self-restraint and self-control. The focus on the self and self-restraint in Elias's work is further amplified when set in the context of the growth in the US of contemporary social theory, including interactional theory, social constructionist theory and social psychological theory. Elias's work was influenced by US social theorists, but he was critical of functionalist theorists such as Talcott Parsons and Robert Merton, but was more positive about Erving Goffman. However, he criticized Goffman for his lack of historical perspective. It was left to a later generation of scholars and theorists, including Arlie Hochschild and others, to further develop the gendered nature of emotions.

As Brooks (2014) notes:

> The emergence in the 1970s and 1980s of a range of theoretical models such as social constructionism and symbolic interactionism, and as they were developed in the work of a range of theorists including James

Averill, Theodore Sarbin, Arlie Hochschild, and Rom Harre in the US, led to what is now described as 'the affective turn' in the social sciences. As Greco and Stenner (2008: 8) note: '… these authors began to stress some of the very different ways in which emotions are played out interactionally amongst people from different cultural backgrounds, and the variety of ways in which they have been made in different historical periods'. (Brooks, 2014: 9)

Hochschild's work highlights the gendered nature of emotional labour and the gendered assumptions operating in organizational contexts. Hochschild uses, as an example, the recruitment and training of flight attendants. Hochschild's work contributes to broader theoretical questions – including the emphasis on social norms and the importance of interaction as a mediating factor between individual personality and social structure, which is an important element of Hochschild's work – and provides a detailed social insight into how norms become embedded into definitions of emotion via interpretive processes which include labelling and attribution. Social interactionism as a sociological theory has, of course, given focus to social norms and patterns of interactionism. Greco and Stenner (2008: 103) show that concepts introduced by Hochschild, including 'emotion work' and 'feeling rules', emphasize the significance of social norms. Underpinning the significance of these concepts is Hochschild's emphasis on connecting emotions to questions of power and social structure, and in addition, 'feeling rules' can be seen as that part of ideology which deals with emotions.

The Elysian school represented in the work of Cas Wouters highlights the absence of an understanding of the gendered nature of emotions in the work of Elias and others. Wouters' (1989) criticism of the work of Arlie Hochschild (1983) has become a classic in terms of what were attempts to establish a theoretical framework for analyzing emotions. Wouters criticized the symbolic interactionist and social constructionist work on emotions and uses Hochschild's (1983) *The Managed Heart* as an exemplar. Wouters maintains that Hochschild '*pretends*' to present a new social theory of emotions, which Hochschild attributes to the classical theorists Dewey, Gerth and Mills, Goffman, Darwin and Freud. He argues that Hochschild hardly considers 'learned, internalized controls of emotions', and Wouters claims that this process of 'learned self-regulation takes the form of a tension balance between emotional impulses and emotion controlling counter-impulses' (Wouters, 1989: 103).

Wouters' critique of Hochschild's model of emotions as developed in the concepts of 'emotional labour', 'emotions work' and 'feeling rules', which Wouters claims draws on a form of Marxism and Goffman's 'dramaturgical perspective', is critical of Hochschild's model of the commercialization of the 'real self' through the organizing and structuring of behaviour. He maintains that Hochschild's analysis is really a critique of capitalism, not more broadly of the commercialization of emotions. In fact, Hochschild, in books such as *The Commercialization of Intimate Life*, focuses on the 'costs' of emotion management and how the commercialization of feeling exacerbates such costs. Wouters also criticizes what he maintains is a false distinction that Hochschild makes between the public and private self in her book *The Time Bind: When Work Becomes Home and Home Becomes Work* (1997). Wouters maintains that this is a false dichotomy, and he argues that public and private selves are based on a continuum as opposed to a dichotomy. Wouters's critique of Hochschild's work has done little to detract from the significance of her work in elevating the analysis of the gendered nature of emotions within an organizational context and more broadly in the social sciences.

Perhaps one of the most significant contributions of Hochschild's work is in the area of political economy and the implications of emotional labour. As Greco and Stenner (2008: 16) note: 'Affect is central to contemporary economic processes, whether in the form of "emotional labour" in the service industry, or "emotional intelligence" in the context of organizational management, or of the increasing attention paid to *feeling* in developing marketing strategies for particular products' [italics added].

Hochschild's work highlights the gendered nature of emotional labour and the gendered assumptions operating in organizational contexts. Hochschild uses, as an example, the recruitment and training of flight attendants. Hochschild's work contributes to broader theoretical questions – including the emphasis on social norms and the importance of interaction as a mediating factor between individual personality and social structure, which is an important element of Hochschild's work – and provides a detailed social insight into how norms become embedded into definitions of emotion via interpretive processes which include labelling and attribution. Social interactionism as a sociological theory has, of course, given focus to social norms and patterns of interactionism. Greco and Stenner (2008:103) show that concepts introduced by Hochschild, including 'emotion work' and 'feeling rules', emphasize the significance of social norms. Underpinning the significance of these concepts is Hochschild's emphasis on connecting emotions to questions of power and social structure, and in addition, 'feeling rules' can be seen as that part of ideology which deals with emotions.

The significance of Hochschild's work is the way in which she illustrates how the sociology of emotions operates as an intervention. As Greco and Stenner (2008: 12–13) maintain, contrary to Wouters's position, 'theories of emotion do not simply hover above their subject matter. Rather they intervene in the affective life they scrutinize.' It is this which distinguishes much of the analysis of contemporary social theorizing from models such as that of Elias. The emergence of emotions in the social sciences and the 'turn to affect' has led to profound transformations in the way social relations are conducted at an individual level and more generally. These theoretical developments are explored later.

In a very useful analysis of the intersection of sociological theory with emotions, Powell and Gilbert (2008: 394–5) provide a fascinating synopsis of how emotion is explained in the work of a wide range of contemporary theorists, from Parsons to feminism and postmodernism.

Powell and Gilbert's analysis is interesting as a result of the breadth of its scope and its drawing on a wide range of contemporary sociological theorists. Powell and Gilbert argue that in contemporary social theory, the role of emotions in social theory has tended to be neglected in considering the work of Parsons and structural functionalism, as well as in Luhmann's (1989) systems theory. In addition, the neglect has also extended to the theorizing of Althusser (1971) and Gramsci (1971). Both theorists are interested in showing people's emotional commitment to ideas and social practices through concepts such as 'interpellation' (Althusser) and 'hegemony' (Gramsci). Both theorists offer imaginative and important explanations of the relationship of emotions and culture. Another theorist who implicitly builds emotions into his analysis is Stuart Hall (1986), who draws on the concept of 'condensation' to explain the intersection of ideas and emotions in cultural representation. All three theorists provide important interventions in understanding emotions in cultural understanding and provide important developments for future theorists in social and cultural theory.

Other major theorists which are drawn on elsewhere include Anthony Giddens, whose work on the emotions and intimacy is well established. Perhaps less well known is his work on ontological insecurity and risk, which embeds emotions into his analysis. In addition, Pierre Bourdieu's work is of course a cornerstone for feminist theory through his analysis of 'habitus', but more broadly his theorization shows how individuals are constantly striving to cope with the emotional demands and contingencies of daily life.

Feminist theorizing is diverse and multi-faceted, as is shown across the chapters of this book, and has contributed significantly to understanding the role of emotions in social theorizing. Within feminist theorizing more generally, emotion is understood as gendered, and for early theorists understood as framed by patriarchy (Marshall and Witz, 2004). Later feminist theorists built on this early thinking and developed the role of emotions more fully in relation to consumption and neoliberalism (Rottenberg, 2014a; Banet-Weiser, 2015).

Emotions have also played an important role in other areas of social theory, including the relationship of discourse and governmentality in managing emotions (Dean, 1994). Postmodernism has also provided valuable additional dimensions to understanding the significance of emotions to social theory. As stated, more recent theorizing has focused on exploring consumerism and desire within contemporary society, which helps to shape individuality.

As the author has noted elsewhere (Brooks, 2014), the work of contemporary social scientists has placed the study of emotions centrally within their analysis. Barbalet (2002) outlines the significance of emotions to sociological analysis, as he notes: 'Once the importance of emotions to social processes becomes clear, the intellectual constitution of sociology and those who have contributed to it, have to be rethought' (Barbalet, 2002: 3).

## Part III. Reflexivity, emotions and identity

Reflexivity is an important concept in contemporary social theorizing. The intersection of reflexivity with emotions and identity also has implications for understanding the embedding of emotions in identity formation. The author has written extensively about social theory and reflexivity (Brooks, 2008, 2010; Brooks and Wee, 2008). Contemporary social theory has been dominated for the last 20 years by attempts to understand social change in relation to global transformations and the growth of individualism. The 'turn to affect' in the social sciences is part of a broader analysis of understanding 'individualization' and society in late modernity.

Sociologists including Holmes (2010), Burkitt (2012) and Archer (2007) have all addressed the intersection of reflexivity and emotion. Holmes's (2010) position in her article 'The emotionalization of reflexivity' is exactly that. She maintains that 'while theories of reflexivity have not entirely ignored emotions, attention to them has been insufficient. These theories need emotionalizing and ... [Holmes] proposes that emotions have become central to a subjectivity and sociality that is relationally constructed' (Holmes, 2010: 139). Burkitt, closely following Holmes, claims that:

> Holmes has convincingly argued that theories of reflexivity have tended to ignore the emotions when considering the ways in which individuals monitor their own behaviour and deliberate about the increasing array of life choices that face them in late modernity, suggesting this means sociologists need to 'emotionalize' theories of reflexivity. (Burkitt, 2012: 26)

Holmes recognizes that there has been considerable debate within sociology about the meaning and importance of reflexivity within the contemporary social world (Giddens, 1990; Beck, 1992; Beck et al, 1994; Archer, 2007). However, she notes that despite this history, the significance of emotions as a dimension of reflexivity has been limited. Holmes (2010: 140) situates the concept of reflexivity at the heart of her thinking about emotions in social theorizing and argues that reflexivity can be seen as an 'emotional, embodies and cognitive process', where individuals attempt to understand their lives and to respond to their social environment and to others through these processes.

One of the main limitations of theories of reflexivity as defined by Beck (1992, 1994) and Giddens (1990, 1992) is the focus on detraditionalization and risk, and the highlighting of fear as a major response to the difficulties of making choices within modernity. Beck uses the example of such a risk as the high risk of relationship break-up, which people cannot protect themselves against. However, as Holmes points out, fear is just one emotion and the 'reflexive modernization' theorists ignore the impact of other emotions on their lives. As Burkitt (2012) observes, Giddens's focus on risk means that Giddens overemphasizes fear and anxiety in modernity and does not recognize that emotions emerge when people face constant change.

Both Holmes and Burkitt usefully draw on Archer (2003, 2007) for a critique of the reflexive modernization theorists such as Beck and Giddens. She is supportive of Beck and Giddens insofar as they are critical of routine action. Holmes (2010: 141) maintains that 'Archer's ideas about agency are helpful in relocating it as a practice of actual human beings living together in the world. This requires departing from Beck, Giddens and associated theorists (see Beck et al, 1994), who conflate structural effects with the powers of individual agents.'

Burkitt draws on Archer's (2003) work where she makes the 'internal conversation' central to reflexivity. So, for Archer, reflexivity is defined as the mental capacity of people to think about themselves in relation to their social context. Burkitt (2012) explains the similarities and divergences between Archer's and Giddens's thinking about reflexivity. Both Giddens and Archer share an understanding of reflexivity which is about deliberation and choice when it comes to objective circumstances. In addition, both share the view that 'the unconscious' provides the route into reflexive consciousness. However, Archer diverges from Giddens in that the unconscious plays a more limited role and is only drawn on to distinguish it from those things which remain non-conscious. Thus, in Archer's thinking and analysis, 'the non-conscious, by definition, can play no part in the conscious, reflective deliberations of the active agent' (Archer, 2003: 25).

Burkitt does however note that Archer's (2003) focus on emotions largely figure in her work only as commentaries, as opposed to a full critique of the reflexive modernization thesis.

## Part IV. 'The emotionalization of reflexivity'

Holmes, in her analysis of the 'emotionalization of reflexivity', argues that emotions are core to reflexive processes, however she notes that:

> Changing social conditions impact across various social spheres and although people draw upon tradition they sometimes face novelty, with feelings of excitement and possibility, not just fear of risk. This

is arguably most evident within intimate life; the sphere in which reflexivity has been expected to involve emotions and concern for others (see Hochschild, 2003), but now within a framework of individual choice (Giddens, 1992). (Holmes, 2010: 147)

Arlie Hochschild's work, as noted, has been groundbreaking in terms of understanding emotions within sociology. As Holmes (2010: 144) observes, 'her concept of emotion work can provide some purchase in establishing the importance of emotions in reflexive practices that are relational (Hochschild, 1983)'. As can be seen across various chapters of this book, Hochschild's work has made significant interventions in understanding emotions within sociology.

Holmes (2010: 144) outlines what she regards as some of the key elements in Hochschild's (1983) work. Emotions are seen by Hochschild as 'sensations' which are largely determined by socially determined rules about how emotions are designated, thus she distinguishes them from 'naturally' occurring physiological events. Secondly, a fundamental concept in Hochschild's work is 'feeling rules', which she maintains are established in the norms of emotional behaviour. In presenting emotions in this way, Hochschild helps us to understand how emotions are shaped by social conditions. Finally and importantly, Hochschild argues that within capitalism, 'emotion work' is seen as becoming increasingly commercialized (Hochschild, 2003) and defined as 'emotional labour' which individuals expend in exchange for a wage or salary.

The implications of the role of emotions as an aspect of reflexivity can be seen across a wide range of sociological fields. As Holmes (2010: 147) shows: 'The emotional and relational element of reflexive practices, is most obvious when they are concerned with love and care, but is evident in work (Hochschild, 2003), class relations (Skeggs, 1997, 2005), political activism (King, 2006), education (Reay, 2005) and no doubt other areas.'

## In summary

This chapter has examined the history of emotions in sociology across a range of socio-historical and theoretical dimensions and explored the significance of emotions in classical and contemporary theoretical perspectives. It explored the relationship between emotion and reason within Enlightenment modernity and how this was addressed by classical theorists. The chapter also looked at a range of contemporary social theorists and in particular looked at the contribution of Arlie Hochschild's work to understanding the emotions in sociology. Finally, the chapter reviewed the relationship between reflexivity and the emotions in contemporary social theorizing and considered 'the emotionalization of reflexivity'.

3

# Privatized Emotions: Emotional Complexity in Late Modernity

## Introduction

Chapter 3 builds on some of the debates outlined in Chapter 2 and focuses on how the late modern era has changed the way we experience and act on our emotions. The chapter demonstrates an increased awareness and experience of emotional complexity in late modernity by challenging the emotional/rational divide. The chapter also reveals tensions between collectivized and individualized–privatized emotions in investigating emotions. Part I of the chapter examines relational complexity in late modernity and examines the work of a number of theorists who have contributed to understanding such relational complexity, including Giddens (1991, 1992), Bauman (2003) and Archer (2012) among others. By relational complexity, we understand the increased emphasis on a 'liberation' from traditional conceptions of relationships and a focus on 'individualization' as discussed by these theorists. Part II of the chapter looks at the relationship between gender and emotional complexity in late modernity, examining different gender responses to emotions such as anger. Finally, Part III of the chapter looks at the complexity of emotions in late modernity, focusing on loneliness and contextualizing this in relation to intimacy and relationships.

## Part I. Relational complexity in late modernity

> Reflexive modernization is a radicalization of – rather than a break with – modernity, and is characterised by the fact that actors are forced to confront and cope with new uncertainties manufactured by the institutions of modernity. (Illouz, 1997b: 51)

This quote from Illouz highlights some of the issues raised by the reflexive modernization thesis as well as reflecting the relational complexity that accompanied it. As is well established, Anthony Giddens (1991, 1992) is one of the key proponents of the reflexive modernization thesis, as Patulny et al (2019) observe. In his argument within the reflexive modernization thesis, Giddens's (1991) point is that Western developed societies are distinctly different from those of the past. In response to the characteristics of neoliberalism, including consumer-oriented economic relationships, Giddens argues that this is paralleled by individuals who can be seen to be increasingly individualized and reflexive (Elliott and Lemert, 2006) and who prefer self-responsibility and freedom. In addition, individuals also prefer self-responsibility over a reliance on traditional forms of authority (Davis, 2008; Archer, 2012).

Holmes (2011: 4) argues that Giddens tends to oversimplify the significance of emotionalization: 'Relational complexity can be difficult to deal with emotionally, as traditional practices fade. The individualization thesis (Bauman, 2003; Beck and Beck-Gernsheim, [1995] 2002; Giddens, 1992) does not entirely capture how behavioural and emotional alternatives expand.'

The complexity of relationships, as understood by Giddens, is captured by Giddens in the value of therapy and the development of 'relationship manuals'. In fact, Hazleden (2004) states that Giddens:

> ... explicitly states that he views relationship manuals as significant social and cultural indicators saying that 'they are texts of our time' in a comparable sense to the medieval manuals of manners analysed by Norbert Elias, or the works of etiquette utilised by Erving Goffman in his studies of the interaction order. (Hazleden, 2004: 202)

This is part of what Giddens identifies as an aspect of a 'therapeutic culture', but there are limitations with Giddens's model of relationships, as Hazleden (2004) notes. Giddens's now famous model of the 'new intimacy' is based on a democratizing of interpersonal relationships which Giddens sees as compatible with 'democracy in the public sphere' (Giddens, 1992: 3). However, it is maintained that his vision is a very particular and limited one which emphasizes neoliberal values including autonomy and individuality over and above mutual support and commonality.

In other words, not everyone has access to the higher order categories of reflexivity and it is a development which is differentiated along the axes of gender, class, ethnicity and nationality. There is little doubt that different orders of reflexivity prevail, related to wealth/poverty, education and media access.

Patulny and Olson (2019: 8), in reviewing the unique characteristics of emotional experiences in what Giddens (1991) describes as the 'late modern era', maintain that the late modern era can also be called 'liquid modernity', 'post-modernity' or 'post-industrial society', which is characterized as having fundamentally porous boundaries and without a definite date separating it from modernity.

Building on this model, Archer (2012) and Bauman (1996) show how the unprecedented pace of change is leading to increased self-reflection. The issue of change is addressed by these theorists, Archer (2012) and Bauman (1996). Both maintain that the unprecedented pace of change demands a higher level of self-reflection. Archer emphasizes the need for continual self-reflection, while Bauman focuses on precarity and fluidity leading to increased emphasis on reflexivity and changes to identity. Both theorists show how the modern problem of identity is to maintain openness when it comes to identity.

In addition, Bauman (2004) and Turkle (2011) draw on broader implications of change and link the characteristics of globalized neoliberalism to technology, in particular digital communication (see Turkle, 2011).

Patulny et al (2019: 2) identify four main emotional themes which they maintain characterize late modernity, including firstly, an increasing awareness of emotional complexity; secondly, a tension between emotions which are individualized and collectivized; thirdly, emotions which are privately consumed; and finally, a greater likelihood of emotions being interpreted at both micro-individual and macro-social scale.

In reflecting on the evolution of emotions from the era of classical emotions, through modern emotions to late modernity, Patulny and Olson (2019: 11) note that even at the end of the classical age there was a growth in complexity in understanding and expressing emotions as an emphasis on '"self-reproach" emotions (Lively, 2008: 927) such as shame, guilt and embarrassment started to become more important for maintaining collective social and moral order …'. In the era of 'modern emotions' there was a greater level of individual control and an acceleration of the 'civilizing' process (Reddy, 2001).

As Patulny and Olson (2019: 12) indicate, as market competition and class-based interdependence increased, the system of manners and emotion norms became more elaborate, as Wouters (2007) noted. He maintains that this reinforcement became the responsibility of the individual. Patulny and Olson (2019) also note that there was also greater scientific and institutional interest in understanding the emotions, so that they could be more easily managed.

In the late modern period, as Patulny and Olson (2019: 13) comment, whether as 'liberating (Giddens, 1991) or atomising (Bauman, 2005), late modern citizens favour individual choice, change, freedom and ultimately self-responsibility rather than compliance to (but also support from) traditional authorities (e.g. church, state, family) (Davis, 2008; Archer, 2012).'

One of the key features of the role of emotions in late modernity is the interrelationship of emotion and reasoning. Illouz (2018) comments on the centrality of reasoning and rationality through consumption of intimate emotional pursuits. As Patulny and Olson (2019: 15) comment on the emotional complexity of late modernity, including new emotions that emerge as combinations of other emotions such as shame and guilt as well as completely new emotions including feelings such as ambiguity (Burkitt, 2002) and 'disconnected ambivalence' (Sennett, 1998; Bauman, 2000).

Perhaps the most significant dimension of emotional complexity is the transformation of intimacy and love (Giddens, 1992; Illouz, 2012, 2018). Giddens (1992) famously asserts that the 'pure' relationship now characterizes relationships in late modernity and that the driving force for these are internal love rather than external material rewards. However, Giddens is not without his critics and other theorists highlight how relationships in late modernity have become temporary and this has been compounded by digital relationships. The implications of this are loneliness and dislocation (see Hookway et al, 2019). Bauman (2005) is also highly critical and argues that in these relationships, love has been replaced by lust as just another sensation. Some argue that the emotion of ambivalence more accurately expresses the complexity of relationships, which means the sensation of experiencing too many feelings at once leading to confusion in feelings.

One of the most interesting dimensions of the individualization of emotions is their commodification. Patulny and Olson (2019: 16) maintain that emotions are more commodified now than in any other era, as they comment: 'Late modern consumption has opened endless opportunities to pursue emotions as commodities such as risk and excitement (Illouz, 2018; Poder, 2008; Zinn, 2006)'. However, they also note that Barbalet (1999) maintains that boredom has also become endemic.

What is clear from an analysis of emotions in late modernity is that there is increasing complexity in both the range and intensity of emotions from 'self-reproach' emotions to mediated emotions. In addition, late modernity is also characterized by a 'therapeutic culture' (Illouz, 2008) and a 'happiness industry' (Ahmed, 2008; Davies, 2015). More than anything else, late modernity encourages us to 'manage emotions as individual consumers', which can lead to more complex emotions such as anxiety, loneliness and ambivalence (see Part III later).

## Part II. Gender and emotional complexity in late modernity

Traditionally and contemporaneously gender has been significant in defining emotions, and women were held to different emotional standards and norms to men and it was generally held that women were naturally more emotional than men.

Lively (2019) makes that point that women were traditionally held to different standards when it comes to emotional experience, expression and management. She states that since the mid-1990s, men are also seen to experience emotions and have also engaged in emotional labour (Pierce, 1995; Simon and Nath, 2004; Jackson and Wingfield, 2013; Cottingham, 2015). However, as Lively (2019: 73) comments, women are likely to be expected to be more caring and nurturing than men, in a variety of different settings, and face situations where they feel obliged to conceal feelings of anger, frustration and irritation through emotional labour. By contrast, men are more likely than women to higher standards of 'affective neutrality' and 'professionalism' (Pierce, 1995; Cottingham, 2015), as well as enjoying higher status shields (Hochschild, 1983; Lois, 2003) which it is argued protects them from misplaced anger from others.

Lively (2019) also notes that it is only relatively recently that research on how gender interacts with other social factors such as 'race' and social class has developed. Durr and Wingfield's (2011) work on African-American professional women and Jackson and Wingfield's (2013) study of Black men in mainly White colleges highlight the significance of intersectionality.

Lively (2019: 74) also looks at research which focuses on emotion and gender outside of the traditional gender binary: 'Schrock, Boyd and Leaf's (2009) analysis of the emotion management strategies of male-to-female transsexuals, documents the emotional pitfalls of passing, as well as temporal aspects of emotion management that, for the most part, had been overlooked in other qualitative studies.'

Simon and Nath (2004), drawing on an earlier General Social Survey, tested cultural and structural theories of emotion and found that once a range of socio-demographic factors ('race', age, education, family income) and social structural factors (employment, marital and parental status) were taken into account, there were few significant differences in women's and men's emotional experience.

*Gender, women and anger*

The one area of significant difference in women's and men's emotions, once structural conditions were held constant, were higher rates of self-reported distress and anger for women. Simon and Nath (2004) note that anger is an emotion which is traditionally associated with males. In addition, they also found significant differences in the way women and men manage their anger. The conversation was shifted in relation to gender and emotions towards a sociological focus to men's emotional experiences which had previously been undocumented. This highlighted the unique and gendered means of emotion management which characterized men's response.

Lively also draws attention to Simon and Lively's (2010) research which examines the relationship between women's more intense and enduring anger and self-reported distress. They found that once the intensity and duration of anger were controlled, that women's higher rates of distress disappeared (Lively, 2019: 76).

A final dimension of this area is the emotional cost of inequity in the home. In work by Lively, Steelman and Powell (2006) they examined how perceived inequity in the household division of labour between women and men had an impact on a range of emotional sites, including pride, tranquility, anger, fear, distress and self-reproach. In addition, Lively (2019) also shows distinctions based on gender related to 'under-benefiting' and 'over-benefiting'. It is maintained that 'under-benefiting' is positively associated with areas such as distress, fear and self-reproach and that men were more likely to experience feelings of anger and rage when they perceived they were experiencing 'under-benefiting'. Women, on the other hand, it is maintained, were more likely to experience emotions such as fear and self-reproach when they perceived they were experiencing 'over-benefiting'.

The focus on Lively's work in this section is important as it focuses on an important aspect of the book, which is the interaction between a range of different factors including gender, 'race' and social class, among others. Her work also challenges categories within traditional gender binaries. Lively's research is also important in exploring the interaction between gender and social structure in the shaping of experience related to the emotions. Lively (2019) provides a sophisticated and nuanced approach to understanding the complex relationships between gender and emotions in late modernity. Lively also maintains that the sociology of emotions emerged with the shift from modernity to late modernity, and she claims: 'it was developed as an attempt to understand how historically specific cultural norms around gender and social structural arrangements shape emotional experience' (Lively, 2019: 79).

## Part III. Complex emotions – loneliness in late modernity

Much has been written about the importance of love and intimacy in late modernity for the sociology of emotions (Giddens, 1992; Jamieson, 1999; Bauman, 2005; see also Chapter 7), but far less has been written about loneliness. As has already been shown, late modernity is characterized by emotional complexity and as Hookway et al (2019: 83) indicate, the complexity is revealed in the recognition that the experience and emotional management of loneliness is shaped by social-structural conditions such as gender and age (Flood, 2005; Stanley et al, 2010; Franklin and Tranter, 2011; Patulny and Wong, 2012). They argue that the situation is also improved by increasing reflexive analysis and new forms of agency.

The backdrop of the transformation of love and intimacy provides a significant site to explore the emotional complexity of loneliness in late modernity. Hookway et al (2019) argue that contemporary theorists such as Bauman (2003, 2007) and Illouz (2012) show that 'loneliness is endemic as intimate relationships become the focus of self-fulfillment and take on an individualistic and consumeristic quality' (Hookway et al, 2019: 84).

In the case of Bauman (2007), his emphasis is on the consumerist drive and he maintains that contemporary relationships have a limited shelf life, which are always vulnerable to change or 'upgrade'. Hookway et al (2019) argue that as a result there is a greater likelihood of loneliness as relationships experience a transformation, with love becoming a site for experiencing sensation and pleasure as opposed to enduring commitment and lifelong relationships.

Illouz (2012) shares Bauman's pessimism in attempting to establish meaningful love bonds in late modernity, particularly for women. Illouz (2012: 247) maintains 'that romantic love in late modernity is not just a cultural ideal, but has become a "social foundation for the self"' (Hookway et al, 2019: 84). Illouz (2012: 163) points out that love is a key site to achieve validation of the self, especially for women who will not have had the same opportunities as men to achieve an identity through career or work. She argues that for women, as a result, there is a never-ending search for romantic love as a cultural ideal. Illouz (2012: 84) maintains that 'ambivalence is a new and defining emotional characteristic of contemporary love relationships.' What is missing from Illouz's analysis is a class-based analysis of this issue. The ability to establish an identity through career or work for women (as for men) is a class-related issue, and middle-class women have much greater capacity for developing an identity through career and work.

Hookway et al (2019), following Bauman (2003) and Illouz (2007), theorize two main ways that emotions of ambivalence in love are transforming the late modern experience of loneliness. In the first instance they maintain that consumer pressure and a more intensive focus on self-scrutiny, which now characterizes intimacy, can lead to greater feelings of restlessness, ambivalence and loneliness within relationships; this, they argue, leads to insecurity and destabilization. Secondly, Hookway et al maintain that ambivalence and lack of commitment may lead to a desire to leave a partner and to move on, but the prospect of loneliness may act to delay any decision. They also point out that while Bauman's (2003) theory of *liquid love* focuses on the constancy of change, it overlooks the fact that some may not choose to move on due to concerns about loneliness. Hookway et al (2019: 85) argue that some people may choose to stay together for the children's sake, but they state that, following Bauman (2003), 'late modern relationships are be-set by an emotional tension between risk and reward.'

Giddens is the spokesperson for a more positive assessment of relationships in late modernity as he suggests less rather than more loneliness as a result of the transformation of intimacy. Hookway et al (2019: 85) observe that in Giddens, the fragility of relationships is not seen as a cause for anxiety or even ambivalence, as Bauman sees it, but Giddens has an optimism regarding changing social conditions and intimacy. Hookway et al (2019) note that Giddens has been the subject of criticism for overstating the opportunities for the emancipation of women from traditional gender roles (Jamieson, 1999). Giddens is also criticized for failing to comment on how 'pure relations' as advocated by Giddens, still benefits men more than women (Illouz, 2012). Hookway et al (2019) also argue that Giddens does deserve attention in how his work addresses the reshaping of relationships in terms of the experiences of loneliness.

There is of course a much wider literature which is critical of the 'reflexive modernization' thesis maintaining that love relationships are increasingly short-term (Smart, 2007; Holmes, 2016). Holmes and Smart argue that intimate relationships have changed but still remain central in people's lives. Hookway et al (2019: 86) maintain that a great deal of empirical research shows that many people do remain in long-term committed partnerships and continue to seek committed and caring relationships (Smart, Neale and Wade, 2001; Holmes, 2016; Hobbs, Owen and Gerber, 2017). They also maintain that the West is still motivated by the idea of 'soul-mate love' (Carroll, 2001).

One of the big developments of late modernity is the proliferation of digital devices and social media platforms in both the development of relationships and in the increasing loneliness of late modernity. Both Bauman (2007) and Turkle (2011/2013, 2015) argue that social media provide a worrying trend that is making us lonelier.

Bauman argues that new communications see connections replace relationships as social bonds become short-term. Similarly, Turkle (2011/2013) makes the point that technology makes it easier to remain apart and offers the illusion of companionship.

In an interesting study by Amichai-Hamburger and Ben-Artzi (2003), the researchers look at the relationship between the internet and loneliness, showing that lonely people use the internet more regularly than non-lonely people; they therefore conclude that lonely people are attracted to using the internet rather than the internet causing loneliness. Hookway et al (2019: 88) show that social media has been shown in other studies (Lopez et al, 2017) to reveal different levels of social inclusion and gratification which is linked to the initial loneliness of the user. There is also evidence that loneliness decreases significantly for those who draw on image-based social media because they provide both 'immediacy' and 'intimacy'.

Thus the landscape of emotions and relationships in late modernity is a complex and nuanced one and across a wide range of theorists and studies a complex and differentiated picture emerges, with little doubt that the nature of relationships is continuing to change and is complex for women and men.

## In summary

As can be seen from the debates raised by this chapter, the 'reflexive modernization' thesis provides an interesting backdrop to consider the development of emotions and relationships in late modernity. On the other hand, the move to 'pure relationships' as a result of the transformation of intimacy is driven by individualization, consumption and self-reflexivity, and can lead to more 'ambivalence' in relationships. This can lead to people becoming lonelier in relationships. However, the move towards 'pure relationships' can also offer the possibility for less loneliness as relationships become more open. The role of digital and social media has become significant in both the development of relationships and in whether they are increasing the possibility of loneliness.

4

# Emotional Intersections: Gender in Emotions

## Introduction

Chapter 4 looks at emotional intersections around gender, which includes feminism. Feminism has engaged fully with emotions and as Ahall (2018: 41) shows, 'a feminist approach to the politics of emotion through gender is about how we become invested in social norms, it is about the affective investments in gender as a social norm.' A wide range of feminist writers and theorists will be considered in this chapter, particularly in the context of 'the affective-turn' in feminist theorizing. This chapter also looks at contemporary feminist perspectives on the emotions and reviews a wide range of contemporary feminist theoretical debates in the area.

Part II of the chapter is concerned with masculinities and emotions. De Boise and Hearn (2017), in an article entitled 'Are men getting more emotional? Critical sociological perspectives on men, masculinities and emotions', have challenged the idea of 'emotional inexpressivity' in men. This chapter will review and analyze a wide range of research on the relationship between masculinity and emotions.

## Part I. Feminist perspectives on emotions – early perspectives – the 'turn to affect'

A wide range of feminist writers and theorists will be considered in this chapter, particularly in the context of 'the affective-turn' in feminist theorizing. Pedwell and Whitehead (2012), in 'Affective feminism: questions of feeling in feminist theory', engage with the relationship between feminist theory and the 'affective-turn'. As Pedwell and Whitehead (2012) comment:

> Feminist scholars have been at the heart of these engagements with affect, in part, because, for some, feminism itself is a politics 'suffused

with feelings, passions and emotions' (Gorton, 2007: 333), but also one that has long recognised the critical links between affect and gendered, sexualised, racialised and classed relations of power. (Pedwell and Whitehead, 2012: 115)

There is a clear divide between 'early' feminist perspectives (Ahmed, 2004, 2010; Gorton, 2007; Hemmings, 2012; Pedwell and Whitehead, 2012), which focused on the 'turn to affect' in understanding gender in emotions, and contemporary feminist perspectives which focus on the relationship between feminism and neoliberalism. This is part of a broader debate on 'the affective, cultural and psychic life of postfeminism' (Gill and Scharff, 2011; Gill, 2017). There are important dimensions of this which include a consideration of the 'confidence culture' (Banet-Weiser, 2015, 2018; Gill and Orgad, 2015, 2017) and its significance in the 'remaking of feminism' (Rottenberg, 2014a; Elias, Gill and Scharff, 2017; Gill and Kanai, 2018; Kanai and Gill, 2020). These broader debates around the 'early' and contemporary dimensions of feminism frame the relationship between gender, feminism and emotions.

Mankekar (2021) makes a distinction between emotion and affect, as she notes:

> Emotion is given meaning through language and conventions of expression and performativity. I conceive of love as an emotion that is experienced and expressed through conventions, attitudes, figures of speech, and behaviors.
>
> Affect, on the other hand, refers to the intensities that generate desiring subjects. Emotion belongs in the realm of the symbolic, while affect is indexical of the ineffable and transformative energy that relays between subjects, and between subjects and objects. (Mankekar, 2021: 3)

Mankekar's concept of affect engages with postmodernist theorists Deleuze (1997) and Massumi (2002), who, she argues, 'insist that affect is distinct from feeling (the domain of linguistics)' (Mankekar, 2021: 2). The distinction is not an easy or accessible one to understand although Mankekar (2021: 10) sets out the distinction clearly. She argues that, like emotion, affect cannot be defined by conceptions of 'interiority'. In other words, affect cannot be located in an individual subject, nor can it be reduced to subjective feelings. Emotion refers to the quality of an experience.

So how do the 'early' feminist perspectives explain 'affect' and the 'affective turn'? Most of these early feminist theorists admit that it is difficult to define 'the affective turn'. Pedwell and Whitehead (2012: 115) recognize the difficulties. They maintain that while the 'affective turn' has become important in feminist thinking, it is still difficult to define, but it has come to signify a range of different movements. It is seen as a 'transdisciplinary intellectual shift' and focuses on an intensification of interest in areas around the emotions and affect which has become elevated to become the object of 'scholarly inquiry' (see Cvetkovich, 2012).

The primary emphasis for these early feminist perspectives was the superiority of reason over the emotional and subjective, but they also recognize the links between 'affect and gendered, sexualised, racialised and classed relations of power' (Pedwell and Whitehead, 2012: 116). They importantly document the wide range of theorists who have focused on affect studies and the theoretical traditions they have drawn on:

> A number of feminists and queer theorists have been highly influential in the field of affect studies, including Ann Cvetkovich (1992, 2003), Judith Butler (1997, 2004), Lauren Berlant (1993, 2007b), Ranjana Khanna (2003), Eve Kosofsky Sedgwick (2003), Teresa Brennan (2004), Sara Ahmed (2004, 2010), Clare Hemmings (2005, 2011), Sianne Ngai (2005). While these critics draw on diverse range of theoretical sources, encompassing Michel Foucault, Karl Marx, Luce Irigaray, Sigmund Freud, Charles Darwin, Raymond Williams, Erving Goffman, Silvan Tomkins and Giles Deleuze, they all explore 'the way feeling is negotiated in the public sphere and experienced through the body' (Gorton, 2007: 334). (Pedwell and Whitehead, 2012: 116)

The emphasis of most of these perspectives is the focus on the reason/emotion binary. This works on the basis that feminist engagement with the politics of affect focuses attention on the way in which feelings can reflect dominant social and political hierarchies in relation to gender, race and sexuality.

Perhaps one of the most successful and accessible of the early theorists of emotion has been Arlie Hochschild. Her work is drawn on at different points in this book and her perspective as a feminist sociologist positions her crucially at the intersection of gender with emotions. Her work anticipates later work by contemporary feminist theorists around the intersection of feminism and neoliberalism.

Hochschild's (1983) classic text *The Managed Heart: Commercialization of Human Feeling* argues that feelings are subject to 'management' both privately and publicly, and that this constitutes 'emotion work' which can be exploited as 'emotional labour'. Hochschild's work, as previously noted, has been hugely significant in building theories of social construction in explaining emotions as well as understanding the gendered, classed, racialized and sexualized relations of power in understanding emotions.

Pedwell and Whitehead draw heavily on the work of Hemmings (2012), who is probably one of the most mainstream advocates of 'affect' within the early feminist theorists. From Hemmings's (2012) perspective, affect is what sustains feminism and gives it momentum. She discusses the politicizing potential of 'affective dissonance' and suggests that politics is what motivates us to something different rather than limiting individuals to what they already know. Pedwell and Whitehead (2012) maintain that Hemmings's commitment to a feminist theorizing of affect can be seen to be in close dialogue with Ahmed (2004).

Hemmings's (2012) primary focus is to establish the connections between feminist knowledge and affect. She introduces the rather obtuse concept of 'affective solidarity'. As Hemmings (2012) comments:

> My own view of affect, in line with Sara Ahmed's and Lauren Berlant's incisive work (Ahmed, 2004; Berlant, 2007b), is that it does indeed offer a way into thinking about the ontological and epistemological, but as a resource for understanding their mutual imbrication or as a kind of knowledge about the interface between ontological and epistemic considerations. (Hemmings, 2012: 149)

The problem with Hemmings's work is that it is punctuated by a language which most readers find incomprehensible and offers no access to understanding theoretical dimensions of affect.

In the case of Ahmed (2004), she (Hemmings) argues for the importance of rage for feminists and cautions against trying to 'domesticate feminist affect' in the face of a critique of feminists as being angry and uncooperative. For Braidotti (1991), it is maintained that it is passion which is key to understanding feminism as transformative. For Braidotti (1991), it is claimed by Hemmings that passion provides both a critique and a way of sustaining feminism, in that it generates both community and pleasure (see also Braidotti, 2006).

Perhaps of greater interest is Gorton's (2007: 333) work, which flags some interesting landmarks in feminism's engagement with women's emotional lives. She shows that in the 1980s feminists including Lila Abu-Lughod (1986), Arlie Hochschild (1983), Bell Hooks (1989), Alison Jaggar (1989), Audrie Lorde (1984), Elizabeth Spelman (1989) and Catherine Lutz (1988) all took an interest in women's emotional lives as well as women's emotional labour.

Gorton draws a distinction between emotion and affect and shows that 'some argue that emotion refers to a sociological expression of feelings whereas affect is more firmly rooted in biology and in our physical response to feelings; others attempt to differentiate on the basis that emotion requires a subject while affect does not' (Gorton, 2007: 334). In order to amplify the distinction, Gorton draws on the work of Elspeth Probyn (2005) and Sianne Ngai (2005) as follows; Probyn, for example, suggests that 'a basic distinction is that emotion refers to cultural and social expression, whereas affects are of a biological and physiological nature' (2005: 11). Ngai, by contrast, discusses 'ugly feelings', and argues that any difference between emotion and affect is not really significant because they are intended to solve the same basic and fundamentally descriptive problem; as a result, 'Ngai uses emotion and affect interchangeably' (Gorton, 2007: 334).

Gorton also shows that one of the areas of central concern in the work on emotion and affect is well expressed in the intrusion of the private sphere. Gorton draws on the significant contribution of Lauren Berlant (1993, 2000) to the debate.

In Berlant's (1993) *The Queen of America Goes to Washington City*, Berlant refers to the 'intimate public sphere' (1993: 4) and elegantly outlines the intersection of the personal and public as follows:

> … the transgressive logic of the feminist maxim 'The personal is the political,' which aimed radically to make the affects and acts of intimacy in everyday life the index of national/sexual politics and ethics, has now been reversed and redeployed on behalf of a staged crisis in the legitimacy of the most traditional, apolitical, sentimental patriarchal family values. Today, the primary guiding maxim might be, 'The political is the personal'. (Berlant, 1993: 177–8; cited in Gorton, 2007: 335)

In a much later work, Berlant (2000), in *Intimacy*, which is a collection of essays which explores the relationship between the intimate and the public sphere, 'goes onto argue that "the inwardness of the intimate is met by a corresponding publicness … At present, in the US, therapy saturates the scene of intimacy, from psychoanalysis and twelve-step groups to girl talk, talk shows and other witnessing genres" (2000: 1)' (Gorton, 2007: 336) (see also Brooks, 2017).

Gorton also draws on another major feminist figure in attempting to understand the public/private divide in exploring the relationship between emotion and the public sphere; this is Elspeth Probyn (2005), and in particular draws on her work on 'shame'. Gorton argues that despite a range of concepts such as hate, paranoia, envy and anxiety, which have been explored by different theorists, shame stands out as important. Probyn (2005), in *Blush: Faces of Shame,* argues for a positive and productive understanding of shame. She argues shame is positive even when it feels bad. Gorton (2007) shows that shame is taken up by both Ahmed and Probyn in their analysis of the performance of reconciliation in Australia (discussed later).

There are quite strong parallels between Ahmed and Probyn. Gorton (2007) shows that in Ahmed's (2004) work on the cultural politics of emotion,

Ahmed draws on a model of what she calls 'affective contagion', where she focuses more on what emotions do and how they circulate than on what they are. One of the emotions is 'disgust', and Ahmed focuses on how this emotion operates and how it racially configures bodies.

The emotion/affect debates are very dense, complicated and frankly unattractive to the average reader. They were developed at a time of second-wave feminism, when feminism was more elitist and dominated by theorists who wrote in a language which didn't touch the lives of ordinary women, including feminists. Fortunately, these theorists have been superseded by a range of contemporary theorists whose work is more accessible to a wider readership of young feminist thinkers. These are outlined next.

## *Contemporary feminist perspectives*

The perspectives adopted by a range of contemporary theorists (Gill and Scharff, 2011; Rottenberg, 2014a; Banet-Weiser, 2015, 2018; Gill and Orgad, 2015, 2017; Gill, 2017; Gill and Kanai, 2018; Kanai and Gill, 2020; Brooks, 2022) also focus on transformation and change, particularly challenging 'hegemonic' Anglo-American feminism. This set of perspectives have a range of characteristics which include individualism, a focus on the self-regulating subject, an emphasis on self-surveillance, monitoring and discipline, and on choice of empowerment.

Part of the debate within contemporary feminist thinking revolves around issues of postfeminism. For those of us who have written about postfeminism as a useful analytical device for years, Gill and Scharff (2011) have the following comments:

> First, it can be used to signal an *epistemological break within feminism*, and marks 'the intersection of feminism with a number of other anti-foundationalist movements including post-modernism, poststructuralism and post-colonialism' (Brooks, 1997: 1). 'Post' as it is used in this sense, implies transformation, and change within feminism that challenges 'hegemonic' Anglo-American feminism 'with its dominant and colonizing voice' (Alice, 1995: 11). In this sense, postfeminism is understood as an analytical perspective and a kind of maturing or 'coming of age' of academic feminism (Yeatman, 1994).
> (Gill and Scharff, 2011: 3)

In addition, the following position is also noted:

> ... postfeminism is also used to refer to an *historical shift after the height of Second Wave feminism*. Tasker and Negra (2007: 1) describe postfeminism as based around 'a set of assumptions, widely disseminated

within popular media forms, having to do with the "pastness" of feminism, whether that supposed pastness is merely noted, mourned, or celebrated'. (Gill and Scharff, 2011: 3)

There are of course critics of this view, including McRobbie (2009) and others, but Gill and Scharff (2011) make some interesting observations in the elaboration of 'postfeminism as a sensibility' (Gill, 2017). As noted, in developing this position, Gill and Scharff (2011: 4) highlight the following dimensions: a move from objectification to subjectification in terms of gender representation of women; secondly, an emphasis on self-surveillance, which includes monitoring and discipline; thirdly, a focus on individualism and empowerment through things like 'the makeover paradigm'; a focus on 'resexualization' of women's bodies; and finally, an emphasis on consumerism and commodification of difference.

Gill and Scharff (2011: 5) extend the debate around postfeminism to links with neoliberalism as follows: they define neoliberalism as a mode of political and economic rationality which is characterized by privatization, deregulation and the withdrawal of the state from social provision. They trace the roots of neoliberalism to the 1980s, which of course came to prominence in the Reagan/Thatcher era in the US and UK. Gill and Scharff cite David Harvey (2005), whose work framed the debates around neoliberalism. Harvey argues that neoliberalism is a theory of political economic practices that views human advancement as best achieved through individual entrepreneurialism and free markets and trade.

Gill and Scharff argue that there is a powerful resonance between neoliberalism and postfeminism, which they maintain is structured by individualism, and, beyond this, they claim that there are parallels between the autonomous and self-regulating subject of neoliberalism and the active 'self-reinventing' subject of postfeminism. They comment that these parallels show that postfeminism is not simply a response to feminism, but go beyond this to show that postfeminism is a sensibility which is, at least in part, constituted through neoliberal ideas (Gill and Scharff, 2011: 7).

Elsewhere, Gill (2017) explores what she describes as 'the affective, cultural and psychic life of postfeminism' and argues that postfeminism is becoming more central across contemporary culture and 'is becoming increasingly dependent upon a psychological register built around cultivating the "right" kinds of disposition for surviving in neoliberal society: confidence, resilience and positive mental attitude' (Gill, 2017: 606) (see also Chapter 5).

There is an intellectual coherence to Gill's analysis of postfeminism, despite the fact that elements of her analysis are overstated. Gill (2017: 607) maintains that the core features of postfeminism include the following elements: the emphasis on individualism and agency; 'the disappearance – or at least muting – of vocabularies for talking about both structural inequalities and cultural influence (Kelan, 2009)'; and the 'deterritorialization of patriarchy' and its subsequent 'reterritorialization (McRobbie, 2009)' in women's bodies as well as in the beauty industry (Elias et al, 2017). In addition, the intensified surveillance of women, including an emphasis on the monitoring and disciplining of the self (Ouellette, 2016), and the focus on the 'makeover paradigm' (Heller, 2007; Weber, 2009) which includes not just the superficial aspects of beauty, but the makeover of one's interior life.

The 'deterritorialization of patriarchy' refers to the removal of male dominance from many aspects of women's lives through the growth of women's rights and social equality more generally. The 'reterritorialization' means the way in which the fashion and beauty industries have exploited women's bodies. This is closely tied into the 'makeover paradigm', which focuses on the transformation of self both externally in terms of appearance but also in terms of one's interior life.

Gill maintains that postfeminism sensibility now suffuses contemporary cultural life, and that it 'increasingly operates in and through the emotions and subjectivity, and thus, might be understood as having an affective and psychic life too' (Gill, 2017: 609). These ideas are developed more fully in Chapter 5.

An important aspect of Gill's (2017: 610) analysis is how she describes 'the affective life of postfeminism' in 'the way it increasingly sets up norms and policies, the kinds of feelings and emotions that are permissible, indeed intelligible (Butler, 1997).' By this she is reflecting on how postfeminism defines both normative structures and policies which impact on individuals' behaviour. In addition, Gill (2017) also maintains that postfeminist culture favours happiness and a 'positive mental attitude', outlawing other emotional states such as anger and insecurity. She maintains that 'the affective, cultural and psychic life of postfeminism' provide a regulatory framework for women in contemporary society. This aspect of contemporary culture is explored in Chapter 5.

Gill maintains that as a result, 'feminism has a new luminosity' (2017: 211). By this Gill means the popularization of feminism (or some might argue, the greater inclusivity of feminism), which includes celebrities, musicians and models proclaiming their 'feminist identities', feminist books topping the bestseller lists and feminist issues appearing in magazines. Banet-Weiser (2015) calls this process 'popular' and Valenti (2014a) calls it 'cool', and Keller and Ryan (2014) talk about feminism having achieved a 'new visibility'. Gill (2017: 211) claims: 'the new visibility of feminism exists in an environment that is at best highly contradictory and at worst profoundly misogynist.'

In addition to its relationship to feminism, postfeminism also has a relationship to neoliberalism. In fact, Gill (2017: 612) sees the link between postfeminism and neoliberalism as establishing 'a neoliberal sensibility' and that this relationship is as well defined as its relationship with feminism. In fact, Gill (2017) says that it can be seen as a 'gendered neoliberalism'. Gill and Orgad (2017) and Gill (2017) argue that many of the 'populist celebrations' have a distinctively neoliberal focus (see also Rottenberg, 2014a).

One of the positive dimensions of postfeminism is the emphasis on intersectional interrogation, which challenges the White, Western, middle-class heterosexual young women emphasis of much traditional feminist discourse. Gill shows that much of postfeminist analysis operates 'non-reductively' in terms of power. However, in their analysis, both Butler (2013) and Gill (2017) are critical of how postfeminism shapes intersectionality.

Butler (2013) identifies a number of celebrities, including Beyoncé, Rihanna, Nicki Minaj and Jennifer Lopez, who she argues can be defined as postfeminist. She contests the rigid drawing of boundaries around 'whiteness' in relation to postfeminism. She argues that while a 'postfeminist sensibility' can be shaped by racial dimensions, women of colour are not outside its definition (see also Gill, 2017).

A major intervention of postfeminism has been the emergence of individualism and the growth of 'confidence culture' (see Gill and Orgad, 2015, 2017) (see also Chapter 5). Gill (2017: 618), drawing on her work with Shani Orgad (2015), has looked at how 'confidence' has become an 'imperative' in contemporary culture. She makes the point that female 'self-confidence' becomes central in the persistence of inequality.

Gill is critical of how women are encouraged through postfeminism to focus on confidence, which is presented as an individual matter, not as a result of structural inequalities. Gill (2017) argues that 'confidence culture' is an example of why it works for subjectivity. She maintains that it is an example of what Foucault (1988) calls a 'technology of self', which operates by establishing a self-regulating process to locate the problems and solutions within women's own psyches.

A number of other feminist theorists have also theorized the link between neoliberal capitalism and feelings, including Eva Illouz (2007) who has dubbed the intersection as 'emotional capitalism'. In addition, Kanai's (2015, 2017) research on *Tumblr* reflects how postfeminism positions women, and how they 'are subject to intensified requirements to demonstrate resilient individuality whilst also enacting a pleasing, approachable femininity' (Gill, 2017: 619). The author has also developed the application of this perspective to the novel *Big Little Lies* by Liane Moriarty (see Brooks, 2022) (see also Chapter 5 for further development).

Gill maintains that postfeminism impacts women in heterosexual relationships, encouraging them to repudiate vulnerability and neediness as aspects of toxic insecurity. As Gill (2017) notes:

> Laura Favaro (2017) and Rachel Wood (2017) both document an increasing focus on 'positive mental attitude' and 'zapping negative

thinking'. Self-doubt and neediness are presented as toxic states, while the notion of 'low self-esteem' has become rendered in some circles as a (classed) term of abuse (O'Neill, 2016; Thompson and Donaghue, 2014). If confidence is the new sexy, then insecurity is undoubtedly the new ugly – at least when it presents in women. (Gill, 2017: 619)

The author develops this discussion and its links with neoliberalism further in Chapter 5.

## Part II. Masculinities and emotions

The field of masculinities and emotions is a largely under-researched field and thus work by de Boise and Hearn (2017) and O'Neill (2015a, 2015b) is hugely interesting and important in developing this field. Interestingly, research by these scholars reflect Part 1 of the chapter in focusing on different theoretical traditions in the field of feminism.

The chapter emphasizes the importance of contesting a single hegemonic masculinity and emphasizes 'masculinities'. As de Boise and Hearn (2017) say:

> Much of this growing body of literature has demonstrated that men both have an understanding of their own emotional lives (Galasinski, 2004) and are more prepared to show emotions in front of other men (Anderson, 2009), leading to a 'softening' (Roberts, 2015) of, or a challenge to, hegemonic masculinity/ies (Lomas, Cartwright, Edgington and Ridge, 2016; Montes, 2013). (de Boise and Hearn, 2017: 783)

De Boise and Hearn show how recent research on masculinity and emotions has drawn on and been influenced by traditional feminist critiques and that 'many men now practice "softer" or "more emotional" forms of masculinity' (de Boise and Hearn, 2017: 779), and, secondly, that 'emotions always influence social action and so need to be better incorporated into sociological accounts of men's behaviour' (de Boise and Hearn, 2017: 779). They draw on what is designated as 'early feminist perspectives' in Part I of the chapter.

O'Neill (2015a, 2015b) on the other hand represents what is called contemporary feminist theorizing and reflects on Anderson's (2009) analysis of 'inclusive masculinity theory', and argues for an analysis of postfeminism with masculinity in order to provide for a fuller explanation of gendered power relations in the formation of critical masculinity studies. Thus, O'Neill's work brings into focus the importance of contemporary feminist theorizing, not just early feminist models of 'affect'.

De Boise and Hearn's research is an important intervention into understanding the relationship between masculinity and emotions. In de

Boise and Hearn's (2017) work, they argue that feminist perspectives have focused on men's emotional lives and getting men to understand their emotions as central in addressing gender inequalities. However, Pease (2012) has argued that 'in studies of gender and emotions, social scientists have tended to suggest that men simply "repress" emotions rather than exploring the ways in which men understand and interpret them, as well as how these connect to social structures' (cited in de Boise and Hearn, 2017: 779).

De Boise and Hearn maintain that a growing body of social research shows that men have an active understanding of their emotional lives and 'practice a more emotional form of masculinity (Forrest, 2010; Holmes, 2015; Roberts, 2013)' (de Boise and Hearn, 2017: 779). They argue that men's emotions can be seen as a feminist issue and that men who are allied to both leftist and feminist movements have responded to calls for taking emotions seriously. As de Boise and Hearn (2017: 779) comment: 'men's relationships with feminist women, globally, through left-wing and civil rights activism, also impacted on attempts to engage men in talking about their emotions as a deliberate consciousness-raising strategy to align themselves with feminist concerns.'

The ability of men to talk about their experiences is important because of the implications for mental health issues. De Boise and Hearn (2017: 782) argue that 'sociologically informed perspectives have noted how men's inability to talk about experiences of vulnerability, mortality, pain, grief and loss (McNess, 2008; Thompson, 1997), in line with cultural gendered constructs, have also been central to their underreporting of depression and other mental health issues.' In addition, they note that 'men's relatively high suicide rates across various different countries have also been explicitly linked to an unwillingness to express or talk about emotions (Clearly, 2012; Garcia-Favaro, 2016)' (De Boise and Hearn, 2017: 782).

De Boise and Hearn show how recent research in the social sciences has focused more on men's emotions, both in terms of men doing more work in heterosexual relationships (Roberts, 2013; Holmes, 2015) and also being more expressive within relationships (Allen, 2007; Forrest, 2010), as well as being more prepared to show emotions in front of other men (Anderson, 2009), which can be seen as leading to a 'softening' (Roberts, 2015) of 'hegemonic masculinities' (Lomas, Cartwright, Edginton and Ridge, 2016; Montes, 2013).

They also argue that some emotions have specifically socially desirable properties which are used to coerce people into normative forms of gender relations. As de Boise and Hearn (2017) observe, even men who are seen to be emotionally expressive and who fall in love can reinforce rather than challenge colonial, patriarchal structures (Illouz, 2012; Jonasdottir and Ferguson, 2013). De Boise and Hearn (2017: 788) show that rather than thinking about emotions as either progressive or regressive for men or women, it is important to consider broader structural issues and to consider how emotions impact on 'neoliberal-capitalist, patriarchal frameworks' which maintain inequalities.

The reservation the author has for the de Boise and Hearn model is its reliance on early feminist models rather than the more dynamic contemporary feminist models around 'consumption' and 'confidence'. However, as it was written and published in 2017 it may have been early in the development of contemporary feminist models. Their summary of the intersection of masculinities and emotions is an important one. They argue that understanding men's emotions is vital on two levels, firstly in understanding gender inequalities and secondly in improving men's well-being and health. They argue that looking at specific emotions as well as clarifying what counts as an emotion may be ways to understand issues of embodiment and motivation in understanding masculinities and emotions.

Another interesting approach to masculinities and emotions is contained in the work of O'Neill (2015a). She explores 'inclusive masculinity theory', postfeminism and sexual politics and provides an interesting new approach to theorizing contemporary masculinities. While de Boise and Hearn focused on early feminist theorizing on affect, O'Neill (2015a: 100) looks at inclusive masculinity theory in relation to postfeminism and innovatively 'consider[s] how inclusive masculinity theory both reflects and reproduces certain logics of postfeminism'. O'Neill states that her 'central concern is the manner in which this scholarship deemphasizes key issues of sexual politics and promotes a discourse of optimism about men, masculinities and social change' (O'Neill, 2015a: 100).

O'Neill's (2015a: 100) work provides an innovative and forward-looking approach to analysis as she argues that 'critical masculinity studies must foreground the analysis of gendered power relations and that the interrogation of contemporary feminism is critical to this endeavour'.

Drawing on Eric Anderson's (2009) *Inclusive Masculinity: The Changing Nature of Masculinities*, O'Neill (2015a: 104) states that Anderson's ethnographic research is based on predominantly White middle-class and upper middle-class university-aged men in the US and the UK. Anderson's main thesis is that recent shifts in the social and cultural landscape have resulted in the development of more 'inclusive' nonhomophobic forms of masculinity. Anderson specifically shows that there has been a decrease in cultural 'homohysteria' or 'fear of being homosexualized', which allows men to develop different forms of masculinity, in particular 'softer', 'more expressive' and 'tactile forms of masculinity'.

O'Neill (2015a: 104) argues that the theory of hegemonic masculinity put forward by Connell (1995), while it describes the way masculinities operate in 'cultures of high homohysteria', becomes increasingly inappropriate in cultures where there is 'diminished homohysteria'. It is claimed that Anderson's (2009) 'inclusive masculinity theory' supersedes the idea of 'hegemonic masculinity' by showing that men are now operating in periods of 'lower homophobia' (Anderson, 2011: 570–1). Anderson maintains that Anglo-American societies are now characterized by reduced 'cultural homohysteria'; in fact, he argues that 'inclusive masculinity' is the empirical and theoretical successor to 'hegemonic masculinity'.

Despite the optimism and apparent inclusivity of Anderson's 'inclusive masculinity theory', O'Neill (2015a: 107) does have reservations with the model, and in her article she goes on to provide 'a critical analysis of inclusive masculinity theory and later relate this to the wider context of contemporary masculinities scholarship'. As O'Neill comments: 'I am less concerned to dispute inclusive masculinity theory on empirical grounds … and am more interested in interrogating the underpinning politics as well as the political effects of this new brand of scholarship vis-à-vis postfeminism' (O'Neill, 2015a: 107).

O'Neill raises some interesting points around Anderson's theory, but perhaps central in this is that it is not the theory of hegemonic masculinity which is flawed for Anderson (2009); in fact hegemonic theory has underpinned some of his earlier work. The point made by Anderson is that the theory of hegemonic masculinities simply doesn't apply to contemporary masculinities. In other words, Anderson doesn't critique the theory of hegemonic masculinities on theoretical grounds, but he contends that social and cultural change in understanding contemporary masculinities has made it redundant. He argues that his investigations of White university-aged men cannot be accounted for within hegemonic masculinity theory. He argues that times have changed and this demands new understandings of gender.

As O'Neill (2015a: 110) observes, Anderson's criticism of hegemonic masculinity theory hinges on the idea that progressive social change has undermined the validity of traditional gendered power relations. As O'Neill comments in assessing Anderson's hegemonic masculinity theory, his analysis is based on a socio-cultural context of the 1980s and 1990s, which is described as an 'epoch of heightened homohysteria', and Anderson commends scholars such as R.W. Connell, Michael Kimmel and Michael Messner for having 'rightly assessed the zeitgeist of their time' (Anderson, 2009: 91), and for building hegemonic masculinity theory into the literature.

Interestingly O'Neill (2015a:111) comments as follows: 'elsewhere referring to these same scholars as masculinity studies' "former leading figures", Anderson seems poised to install himself and other proponents of inclusive masculinity theory as the forebears of a new direction in masculinity studies. This kind of generational logic is accompanied by the supposition that new directions in the field must be, indeed *can only be* forged by young scholars.

The author does feel a sympathy towards Anderson's analysis as she feels it shares the author's critique of early feminist theorizing. However, the author does agree with O'Neill's (2015a: 111) commentary on homophobia in saying that 'though homophobia is heavily imbricated with masculinity, this is *not* to say that homophobia is *the* definitive expression of masculinity'.

O'Neill (2015a) also correctly notes that:

> It is not that Anderson (2009: 98) overlooks the regulatory force of heterosexuality and heteronormativity in social constructions of masculinity; rather, he argues that 'Heterosexism is an independent and unrelated variable for the operation of inclusive masculinities.' In this way, Anderson foregoes any consideration of the gendered power relations of heterosexuality, despite evidence that sexual access to women's bodies continues to play a key role in the organization of masculine subjectivities and men's practices (Pascoe, 2007; Richardson, 2010). (O'Neill, 2015a: 111)

The author agrees with O'Neill's critique of Anderson's observations of young men and their *inclusivity*, as Anderson (2009) observes:

> One can easily see how today men are permitted to carry one-strapped bags. One can easily see the sexualization of bodies in advertising. One can see the increasing demands that men dress sharp. One can see the items, colours, and behaviours once heavily associated with the purchasing power of women, have been marketed to men. (Anderson, 2009: 160, cited in O'Neill, 2015a: 114)

O'Neill is correct in observing how superficial this analysis is, as:

> Anderson is arguing that simply by *looking* at young men it is possible to see that they are now more inclusive. Sorely lacking here is any critical analysis as Anderson takes it for granted that because young men *look* different, they must somehow *be* different, and that this difference is necessarily a good thing. (O'Neill, 2015a: 114)

O'Neill goes on to comment that the '… defiant, celebratory tone Anderson invokes seems to echo the triumphant voice with which postfeminism reclaims all that feminism has disallowed. It is, really, as if "postfeminism has come true" (Gill and Donaghue, 2013) – and not just for the girls!' (O'Neill, 2015a: 114).

O'Neill is correct to show how little research has been undertaken at the intersection of masculinities and postfeminism, as the work by de Boise and Hearn indicates. O'Neill says that in looking through the journal *Men and Masculinities* she could find little in the literature. She identifies work in the area of feminist cultural studies scholars as being one of the few areas where there is scholarship on masculinities and postfeminism, for example, Gwynne and Muller (2013), *Postfeminism and Contemporary Hollywood Cinema*. The author agrees with O'Neill (2015a: 15) that 'to interrogate postfeminism, to take it as an object of analysis, is to ensure that an appreciation of gendered power relations is held in theorizations of men and masculinities, social change and contemporary culture.'

## In summary

This chapter has covered a wide-ranging review of emotional intersections, in particular of gender in emotions. In reviewing the field, the author has considered 'early' feminist perspectives on emotions, in particular exploring the 'turn to affect'. Drawing on a wide range of theorists, the author then moved on to consider contemporary feminist perspectives and explored the relationship between emotions, postfeminism and neoliberalism. The second part of the chapter reviewed some of the research in the field of masculinities and emotions and examined some of the key theorists in the field.

5

# Emotional Capital and Emotional Commodities

**Introduction**

Chapter 5 looks at a broad range of emotional intersections with class, which has played an important part in understanding emotions. The chapter is divided into three parts. The first part considers traditional conceptions of emotional capital and social class, where the focus of this early work drew on the work of Pierre Bourdieu and his analysis of capital. Pierre Bourdieu's (1984) *Distinction: A Social Critique of the Judgement of Taste* is crucial in understanding emotions. The importance of this perspective highlights the link of cultural capital and emotional capital. While Bourdieu's work emphasized gender, he did not refer to emotions explicitly or to 'emotional capital'. While class is important in understanding emotions, it is also the intersection of gender and class in understanding emotions which is significant. The author reviews the work of some of the key feminist theorists: Storr (2002); Reay (2004) and Skeggs (2010), who in different ways develop work around class, emotions and emotional capital.

Part II of the chapter, 'emotions, consumption and commodities', shows how this work has moved on to discussions of emotions, consumption and commodities (Illouz, 1997a, 2009, 2018; Cabanas and Illouz, 2016) through the work of a range of feminists and cultural theorists. Part III of the chapter looks at the further development of the work, through the intersection of capitalism, neoliberalism and the 'confidence culture', reflected in the work of an exciting range of contemporary feminists, including Illouz (2007); Rottenberg (2014a); Banet-Weiser (2015); Gill and Orgad (2015, 2017); Gill and Kanai (2018); Kanai and Gill (2020).

## Part I. Traditional conceptions of emotional capital and social class

In recent years, discussions about social class and emotional capital have moved on to debates around neoliberalism, consumption and the 'confidence culture'. However, it is worth reviewing some of the important feminist research (Storr, 2002; Reay, 2004 and Skeggs, 2010 among others) that anticipated these later conceptual and theoretical analyses.

Reay (2005), in 'Gendering Bourdieu's concept of capital: emotional capital, women and social class', focuses on the intersection of class and emotions. There are also a range of intersecting studies which incorporate this perspective, including Skeggs's (2009) 'The moral economy of person production: the class-relations of self-performance on 'reality' television.'

Much of this early research drew on the work of Bourdieu (1984) and his analysis of capital. Reay (2004) offers an important analysis of Bourdieu, gender and emotional capital. She shows that while Bourdieu deals extensively with gender differences in his work, he does not link these to emotions and never refers explicitly to emotional capital. However, as Reay (2004) shows, '... he [Bourdieu] does describe practical and symbolic work which generates devotion, generosity and solidarity, arguing that this work falls more particularly to women, who are responsible for maintaining relationships (Bourdieu, 1998: 68)'. Reay shows how emotional capital may be understood as gendered capital, in particular through examining the impact of social class on gendered notions of emotional capital.

In his work on *Masculine Domination*, Bourdieu (2001: 77) maintains that 'it has often been observed that women fulfil a cathartic, quasi-therapeutic function in regulating men's emotional lives, calming their anger, helping them accept the injustices and difficulties of life'. Thus, while not directly addressing gender and the emotions directly, Bourdieu's comments highlight important points of intersection in gender and emotions.

Bourdieu's conceptual framework has drawn on Nowotny (1981) in developing the concept of emotional labour. As Reay (2004) states, Nowotny 'saw emotional capital as a variant of social capital, but characteristic of the private rather than the public sphere' (Nowotny, 1981).

In an interesting analysis of Nowotny's perspective, Reay (2004) argues that Nowotny (1981) saw emotional capital as a resource which women have in greater abundance than men, unlike other forms of capital including economic, cultural, social and symbolic, which it is argued have been theorized in ungendered ways. Nowotny raises the question of why women have only been able to accumulate certain kinds of capital and not others, and in addition why have they not been able to convert this capital into other types.

Reay (2004) shows how Illouz's (1997a) early work provided an important commentary on the intersection of gender and emotional capital. Illouz (1997a: 56) argues that

> the ability to distance oneself from one's immediate emotional experience is the prerogative of those who have readily available a range of emotional options, who are not overwhelmed by emotional necessity and intensity, and can therefore approach their own self and emotions with the same detached mode that comes from accumulated emotional competence. (cited in Reay, 2004)

Reay (2004) makes the point that there are clear class differences for women in relation to emotional capital. She argues that it was primarily working-class women who did not have a positive personal experience of schooling and who had difficulty in generating resources of emotional capital for their children to draw on, should they experience difficulties in school.

Skeggs (2010: 37) provides an interesting analysis of the intersection of intimacy and class and draws on Elizabeth Bernstein's (2007) excellent study of class and sex work in the US. Bernstein's study of class differences in sex work in the US maintains that the relationship may not be straightforward. Bernstein shows how middle-class men who pay for sex find working-class women's definition of sex-related tasks disturbing. For example, '$5 for a kiss, $10 for a blow job etc', and they prefer to establish 'a faux form of intimacy' where they attempt to become intimate through talk at the same time as performing sexual acts. Bernstein maintains that male professional high-tech workers do not want to establish relationships of obligation and responsibility and as a result see it as essential to pay for intimacy.

Skeggs shows how Bernstein's research focuses on the role of affect in shaping different forms of exchange: 'The middle-class men prefer the simultaneous mystification of their exchange relationship (pretending that their purchase of sex is less brutal than mere financial exchange (that they are under no obligation of any kind)' (Skeggs, 2010: 37). In addition, Bernstein's research shows how affect shapes different types of exchange; in other words, middle-class men attempt to demystify their 'exchange relationship'. As Skeggs indicates, 'Bernstein's men want their exchange relation to be recognized (no responsibility) *and* misrecognized (not bare exchange), and this can only happen if the women have the appropriate cultural capital (talk plus intimate performance)' (Skeggs, 2010: 37).

Skeggs also references the work of Wilson (2010) who maintains that some Western men use Thai sex bars to establish interactions that, it is claimed, are more human than they can establish at home. Skeggs (2010: 38) maintains that Wilson categorizes this attitude 'as a particular mode of racial and gendered post-Fordist desire'. By post-Fordist desire, Wilson means the way in which contemporary capitalism works through feeling rules, in other words, how social norms work through emotions. In this particular context, Wilson is showing the racial and gendered distinction between Western men and Asian women in the expression of feelings, desire and intimacy. There is of course a power distinction here which is central in post-Fordist analysis of the workplace and of emotions.

In addition, Illouz (2003, 2007) shows how misery has become a highly marketable commodity on talk television. This has reached new heights of late with the Harry and Meghan Netflix debacle, and prior to this with the Oprah Winfrey 'racism' interview with the couple.

Storr (2002), in an article entitled 'Classy lingerie', draws on research on Ann Summers' 'home shopping parties at which lingerie, sex toys and other personal products are sold in the UK'. Drawing on the work of Bourdieu and Skeggs, she (Storr, 2002) maintains that the private world of lingerie is part of a more public world of class distinction. She argues that working-class and lower middle-class women draw on 'mass-market lingerie' to distinguish themselves from upper-class or 'posh' women who they see as 'pretentious, boring, snobbish or tasteless'.

Storr raises the question of what social class has to do with underwear. She draws on the superb work of Elizabeth Wilson (1985), whose socio-historical analyses have done much to provide the historical detail necessary for analysis. Storr (2002) points out that underwear as understood today did not develop until the 19th century, or in the case of the bra until the early 20th century. As Storr shows, for Wilson, the point about underwear is not so much what it *does,* but what it *means*. Wilson (1985) puts the issue of underwear in the wider context of the relationship between fashion, capitalism and modernity:

> For fashion, the child of capitalism, has like capitalism, a double face [...]. We live as far as clothes are concerned a triple ambiguity; the ambiguity of capitalism itself with its great wealth and great squalor, its capacity to create and its dreadful wastefulness; the ambiguity of our identity, of the relation to self, to body and self to the world, and the ambiguity of art, its purpose and meaning. (Wilson, 1985: 13–15)

In addition, for Wilson (1985: 107) herself, 'the distinction between underwear and outerwear reflects the distinction between the public and the private [... and] parallels the late 20th century ambiguity surrounding privacy, intimacy and sexuality.'

## Part II. Emotions, consumption and commodities

Part II of the chapter focuses on the work of Eva Illouz (2009, 2018) in considering the development of the relationship between emotions and consumption. Illouz (2009) sees emotions as a category of consumption and draws on the postmodern sociologist Baudrillard in his analysis of consumption and 'desire'.

Illouz (2009: 382) shows how emotion is better than other concepts in explaining how consumption is positioned: 'between cognition and culture on the one hand and motivational structure of drives on the other.' She has long been concerned with the psychological as well as the sociological dimension but ultimately sees emotion as both cultural and social. She argues that emotion is less a psychological entity than it is a cultural and social one, as individuals enact cultural definitions of personhood through emotion and this is expressed in concrete relationships with others. In other words, emotion is about where one stands across a range of social relationships.

Illouz maintains that emotions contain cognition but that doesn't necessarily entail self-consciousness. She draws on Martha Nussbaum's (2001) important contribution in *Upheavals of Thought: The Intelligence of Emotions* on the issue of 'cognitive appraisal', which she shows: 'need not all be the object of reflexive self-consciousness' (Nussbaum, 2001: 126). She (Nussbaum) goes on to say that 'emotions look at the world from the subject's own sense of personal importance or value' (Nussbaum, 2001: 33).

Building on this, Illouz (2009: 386) argues that emotions are central in the consumer market because they work to 'prioritize references'. This is because the market is 'saturated' with endless choices, and emotions assist in the ranking of priorities by consumers based on emotional choices.

Elsewhere, in her extensive range of work on emotions and intimacy, Illouz (1997a) argues that romantic feelings and bonds are produced and sustained by the invisible presence of a variety of leisure commodities. She states that at the turn of the 20th century, the nascent consumer market channeled and transformed definitions of romance and love, and leisure goods and services such as movies and restaurants provided symbolic outlets to channel and ritualize romance.

Illouz maintains, following Nussbaum (2001), that consumption is structured by emotions in at least two ways, a distinction between background and situational emotions. A background emotion is an emotion that is structurally embedded in a culture of consumption; a situational emotion is attached to a particular context and situation. Illouz (1997a: 389) states that 'situational emotions refer less to the structural properties of the culture of consumption than to the immediate contextual features in which the activity of consumption occurs.'

Drawing on McCracken's (1991) analysis of the expansion of the new consumer market in 16th-century England, Illouz (1997a: 392) notes that McCracken has suggested that the early consumer boom of the 16th century was stimulated by the competition and rivalry among the Elizabethan nobility. McCracken points out that the nobility became dependent on royal favours for survival which meant they had to spend more. This meant these noblemen left their local area to go to court in London where they found themselves in competition with others for the queen's attention and favours. Hence the emergence of a competitive consumer market.

The overlap between emotion and economics can be seen in a number of concepts, and central in this is the concept of confidence as developed by Barbalet (2004). In this context Barbalet sees confidence as an emotion, not simply a 'feeling' or 'affect'. As Barbalet claims, 'confidence arises from acceptance and recognition in social relationships' (Barbalet, 2004: 87) and from the feeling that one is wanted. As Barbalet put it, 'confidence is an emotion through which a possible future is brought into the present' (cited in Illouz, 1997a: 396).

Illouz (1997a: 403) shows that the market for luxury goods expanded in the 18th century as the ranks of the middle and upper classes swelled. She also notes that a significant proportion of these luxury goods that were 'desired during the 18th century were exotic … and were characterised by the fact that they exerted particularly powerful; sensorial stimuli'.

In a later work, *Emotions as Commodities: Capitalism, Consumption and Authenticity*, Illouz (2018) shows that far from heralding a loss of emotionality, capitalist culture has on the contrary been accompanied with what Illouz (2018: 5) describes as: 'an unprecedented intensification of emotional life with actors self-consciously pursuing and shaping emotional experiences for their own sake (Ahmed, 2010; Hardt and Negri, 2006; Hochschild, 1983; Illouz, 2007).' Illouz (2018) shows that in the second half of the 20th century, emotion has figured centrally in people's personal lives, with emotional fulfilment becoming a preoccupation of the self in people's lives.

She claims that emotional life and consumer acts have become inseparably intertwined with each other and calls this process 'the co-production of emotions and commodities'. Illouz (2018) argues that if both rationality and emotionality have become embedded in the 'cultural organization of capitalism', it needs to be explained how capitalism has integrated these conflicting features within the contemporary consumer. Illouz draws on a range of classical and contemporary sociological and cultural theorists including Simmel ([1903] 2004), Weber (1978), Horkheimer and Adorno (1979), Habermas (1985), Smelser (1998) and Welcomer et al (2000) to locate issues of emotion and rationality in broader cultural studies debates.

Drawing on Boltanski and Chiapello (2007) among others, Illouz (2018) argues that there has been a general 'emotionalization' of the workforce, a transformation in the evaluation of criteria regarding emotional satisfaction and 'emotional expressiveness', which she maintains is part of the 'history and sociology of capitalism'. This, Illouz maintains, is part of how emotion is positioned centrally within the general economic process (see Illouz, 2008; Cabanas and Illouz, 2016).

In fact, Illouz goes further and makes the bold claim that 'consumer capitalism has increasingly transformed emotions into commodities and it is this historical process which explains the intensification of emotional life' (Illouz, 2018: 10). She argues that this explains the intensification of emotional life in Western capitalist societies in the late 19th century and second half of the 20th century. This is an important development in Illouz's work, as it understands the relationship between capitalism, consumption and emotions as an interactive one.

Illouz looks at the formation of the consumer sphere, which she shows was accompanied by a new conceptualization of the consumer. Illouz (2018) argues that the growth of consumer culture is not a one-dimensional process where the market supply tried to adapt itself to the consumer where the consumer's needs were pre-existent. Rather, the market shaped the consumer in the image of the goods it was producing. In addition, Illouz shows that those in advertising and marketing deliberately selected strategies which increased the emotional and symbolic value of goods, which Illouz identifies as 'branding'. She says that 'emotional branding' has become a common marketing tool and has become important in conceptualizing the consumer and consumption process by people working in marketing and advertising professions (Illouz and Benger, 2015).

The key emotions used in 'branding' are positive emotions such as love, romance, lust, optimism, cheerfulness, coolness and self-confidence. This is interesting, particularly in the light of 'the confidence culture' as outlined later. Illouz (2018) makes the point that it is not the case that advertising and marketing recognized a 'reservoir of real emotions', but gave goods an emotional meaning, whereby those involved in marketing acted to construct the consumer as an 'emotional entity'. Illouz argues that this makes consumption into an emotional act and at the same time confirms the consumer as being driven by emotions.

Illouz argues that historical and sociological analyses have contributed much to our understanding of consumption as a social and semiotic act, yet when it comes to understanding emotions they have omitted a crucial aspect: 'the historical dynamic of capitalism; its capacity to create *emotions as commodities*' (Illouz, 2018: 13).

She maintains that the concept of 'affective capitalism' which is based on Negri's (1999) concept is important, as is the claim that 'affect is reintegrated within the "fold" of capitalism itself. Meaning, affect and affection are extensively organized, produced and maintained for the needs of capitalism (Karppi et al, 2016)' (Illouz, 2018: 14). Despite this, Illouz argues that the concept of 'affect' remains vague. Illouz claims that the concept of '*emodity*' clarifies the central process of affective capitalism since it connects emotional experience and commodity.

In an interesting analysis, Illouz (2018: 16) shows how Hardt and Negri's (2006) work builds on that of Hochschild (1983). In her study *The Managed*

*Heart,* Hochschild focuses on the 'feeling rules' that workers increasingly resort to, to manage their emotions within corporate structures. Hardt and Negri (2006) go further than Hochschild in seeing 'the production of informational, cultural, symbolic and emotional commodities as mobilizing workers' true emotional capacities and inclinations.'

Illouz (2018: 16) argues that a range of transformations in social and cultural life which include the intensification of private life, particularly around relationships, the definition of self-hood as it applies to 'emotional authenticity', the emphasis of emotional labour in terms of corporate and economic environments and the 'objectification of emotions through knowledge systems'. Illouz maintains that these processes create the framework for development of 'the processes of production of emotional commodities'.

The final important point made by Illouz is her recognition of one of the most damaging aspects for women around the growing emphasis on the emotions, and that is the growth of the psy-industries in late modernity. As Illouz (2018) shows, the implications of the growth of a range of psy-industries targeting the emotions have important implications for mental and emotional health and well-being, as well as 'an ideal emotional make-up' (see Illouz, 2008). Illouz (2018: 20) identifies a range of related groups and processes, including 'psychologists, new age therapies, workshops, self-help books, coaching, and psychiatric medications', which she argues offer expert knowledge and in the process effect emotional change. Illouz argues these include the reduction of stress, anger management, intimacy control, enhancement of self-confidence and self-esteem and reduction of feelings of worthlessness and powerlessness. While these may seem obvious, the strength of Illouz's work is her grounding of social theory in real world outcomes.

## Part III. Capitalism, neoliberalism and the 'confidence culture'

The final section of this chapter focuses on the shift in emphasis within feminism from the second-wave feminist focus on 'affect' to contemporary feminist theorists' emphasis on 'confidence culture'. The discussion of feminist theories of 'affect' have been comprehensively documented earlier in the book. The focus here is on contemporary feminist theorists' focus on 'confidence culture'. The distinction between these generational and cultural understandings has been called by some, 'feminist culture wars'.

In their analysis of the 'confidence culture', Gill and Orgad (2015) look at 'confidence as a technology of self' and argue that as a new technology of self, it brings into existence new subjectivities or ways of being. Within the feminist 'culture wars', Gill and Orgad (2015) argue that the new cultural prominence given to 'confidence' can be considered in various ways. It can be considered as a 'turn to confidence' or a 'confidence movement', or a 'new zeitgeist' or as Garcia-Favaro (2016) calls it, 'confidence chic'. Gill and Orgad argue that it is a discursive formation, and a set of knowledges which produce a 'novel technology of self' which introduces new subjectivities.

They draw on the work of Michel Foucault, particularly his later work and its link to theorizing agency, as they point out that Foucault's later work opened up a space for theorizing agency as well as considering what Butler (1997) calls 'the psychic life of power'. They maintain that there have been a number of productive feminist attempts to develop this focus on 'technologies of selfhood' within the work of a number of theorists, including Teresa de Lauretis (1987), Judith Butler (1990), Susan Bordo (1993) and Angela McRobbie (2009).

Perhaps most importantly, Gill and Orgad (2015: 327) show how the psy-sciences with their 'self-improvement' therapeutic cultures are utterly devastating for women. They claim that this therapeutic model emphasizing healing and recovery, which implies that women need psychological intervention, may be displacing earlier models of feminist intervention which are more political. They make the point that possibly the key factor in the confidence model is the way it has become depicted as a 'feminist turn', as this 'technology of self-confidence' seems to be reformulating feminism itself.

The focus of the critique offered by Gill and Orgad (2015, 2017) is, as noted elsewhere, on two American books, *Lean In* (2013) by Sheryl Sandberg (see Brooks, 2019b) and *The Confidence Code* (2014) by Katty Kay and Claire Shipman. They (Gill and Orgad, 2015: 329) maintain that these books, and it can also be applied to books like them, produce a set of strategies which are geared towards 'gender diversity' in the workplace and more generally towards gender equality.

The focus of both of these books is White, middle-class, professional women, but Gill and Orgad (2015) also show that the US Black Career Women's Network,

> which is 'dedicated to the professional growth of African-American women' defines the black career woman as 'a black woman who is confident and tenacious' who notwithstanding the challenges she encounters 'continues to uphold a positive attitude and image, build a network, pursue professional development, education and mentoring to accomplish her goals'. (Gill and Orgad, 2015: 329)

Gill and Orgad argue that this 'feminist technology of confidence' is systemically reconfiguring feminism and making it safe for a corporate and neoliberal culture. They don't explain why this is a bad thing but seem to feel that feminism and corporate culture are incompatible. The critique of positions adopted in *Lean In* and *The Confidence Code* reflects a wider culture of confidence, as Gill and Orgad (2015) note:

> The focus on confidence is partly predicated on the supposedly 'pragmatic' view that masculine domination and gender inequality are virtually impossible to challenge at the structural level … and, thus, the only way to challenge them effectively is for women to internalize both the responsibility for the problem and the program required to resolve it. (Gill and Orgad, 2015: 330)

Catherine Rottenberg (2014a) also critiques Sandberg's position in *Lean In*, where she notes: '*Lean In* represents a shift "from an attempt to alter social pressures towards interiorized affective spaces that require constant self-monitoring"' (Rottenberg, 2014a: 424). As McRobbie (2013) shows, 'nothing at all is said about material issues like the absence of paid maternity leave for women in the USA, or the need for employer-based childcare' (cited in Gill and Orgad, 2015: 333).

For Gill and Orgad, Rottenberg and many feminists, the emphasis on changing women's psyches as part of the 'confidence culture' is a renouncement of feminism as they understood it: 'Thus the confidence culture "recuperates" feminism by recasting it in its own postfeminist and neoliberal terms as an individualistic, entrepreneurial project that can be inculcated by the self' (Gill and Orgad, 2015: 341).

The implications for feminism, as outlined by Gill and Orgad, are clear. Following Boltanski and Chiapello (2007), the confidence culture allows capitalism to establish itself as a 'new spirit'. They argue that this encourages women to 'makeover their psychic lives' and in the process to makeover feminism itself. This is identified by Gill and Orgad (2015), Rottenberg (2014a) and others as 'neoliberal feminism', which they maintain is complicit with capitalism rather than critical of it.

Elsewhere, Gill and Orgad (2017) make a number of additional related points, as follows. In this article, Gill and Orgad extend their critique to Anne-Marie Slaughter's (2015) work (see also Brooks, 2019b). She argues that it is not sufficient to tell women they need ambition and confidence, but they also need to 'relinquish' aspects of domestic drudgery in order to flourish at work.

In terms of how Gill and Orgad (2017: 22) view Slaughter's perspective, they claim that Slaughter (and others) see heterosexual men as enthusiastic about sharing domestic and caring responsibilities but are being discouraged by women who do not want to relinquish domestic responsibilities. They claim that Slaughter's article for *Time Magazine*, entitled 'Women are sexist too', which Gill and Orgad argue acknowledges inequalities in gender, locates the requirements for change in women themselves and not in the structures of domination in society.

The issue of 'confidence' is seen in the context of popular as opposed to academic feminism, seemingly implying that 'elite' academic feminism is the real feminism and the focus on popular or 'populist' feminism is false consciousness. Gill and Orgad (2017: 25) define the terms as follows; they argue that confidence is important to heterosexual women because it is seen as sexy and appealing to men. They cite *Glamour* magazine, which maintains that men agree that a 'confident, secure, optimistic and happy woman is easier to fall in love with than a needy neurotic one'. It goes on to argue that men are drawn to confident women and they claim this is more important than issues of weight, size or appearance. It appears to be the case that it's about 'making the most of your assets', about emphasizing the right positive mental attitude.

Gill and Orgad (2017: 26) argue that confidence culture appears to be both 'post-queer' and 'post-racial', and as an example of this they draw on Anna Sofia Elias's (2016) work which shows that body love campaigns such as the Dove 2015 'Love your Curls' campaign are directed at Black and mixed-heritage women.

The focus on 'post-queer' and 'post-racial' is extending 'confidence exhortations' beyond the White heterosexual subject by targeting Black and mixed-heritage women. The focus is on 'girls and young women ... constructed as suffering from feelings of inferiority and lack of self-worth – a problem they are cajoled to "fix" through following a series of simple "steps", almost identical to those offered in numerous other confidence-building outlets' (Gill and Orgad, 2017: 26). As Gill and Orgad show, while the suggestions might address specific cultural dimensions, for example, differences in hair types or complexion, most of the suggestions are generic. Thus, as they note, confidence is offered as a 'one-size-fits-all matter'.

Gill and Orgad also state that beyond this, the idea of insecurity and a lack of confidence is both 'abject and abhorrent'. They claim that if confidence is the new sexy, then, for women, insecurity is the 'new ugly'. O'Neill (2016) also confirms this position and argues that self-doubt and lack of confidence are seen as 'toxic states', while the idea of 'low self-esteem' is seen in some circles as a term of abuse.

Despite the criticism of the concept of 'confidence culture', it is recognized that it has offered feminism 'a new luminosity' in popular culture (Banet-Weiser, 2015, 2018). This 'new luminosity' in aspects of popular culture includes the following: feminist books which top the bestseller lists; feminist issues in magazines; the fact that celebrities, politicians and so on identify important issues for feminists and women more generally, including unequal pay and sexual harassment. As Valenti (2014a) comments, feminism is becoming 'popular', 'cool' and achieving a 'new visibility' (cited in Gill and Orgad, 2017: 28).

Valenti raises an interesting question about the new popular feminism; she comments as follows: 'when everyone is feminist, is anyone?'. Gill and Orgad (2017) attempt to assess what the current state of popular feminism has to offer feminism as a movement for self-transformation. They maintain that as wealthy celebrities attach their name to feminist credentials (see Brooks, 2022) and as corporate leaders produce 'feminist self-help guides', the question has to be raised as to whether feminism has simply become an aspect of 'style identity', devoid of a commitment to social transformation. They also raise the question of what does this mean for the future of feminism.

Some feminists have maintained that there are close parallels between postfeminism and the new popular feminism which focuses on a number of characteristics. These include an emphasis on individualism, with agency as a dominant feature of this; the absence of an analysis of structural inequalities; the 'deterritorialization' of patriarchal power and its emphasis on the beauty industry focusing on women's bodies; and the focus on the 'makeover paradigm' in the process of disciplining women's bodies (see Brooks, 2022).

Despite the criticism offered by Gill and Orgad and others to this new popular feminism, they do recognize that it offers an inclusivity which earlier versions of feminism did not, and that the 'target user' is '"every woman" across race, class, age, sexuality and location' (Gill and Orgad, 2017: 29). However, they note there are limitations to the inclusivity of the model.

For example, it is claimed by Gill and Orgad (2017) that the 'confidence culture' has what they call a 'post-racial' tone. This is because women of colour are treated in a highly standardized way which ignores feminism's recognition of social difference, particularly racial difference. It is argued that rather than focusing on the specific needs of different groups of women, which include the need to address anti-racist critiques, the confidence culture flattens difference and the possibility of different levels of critique. A further critical dimension that is identified is the way in which, as Gill and Orgad (2017) maintain, the confidence culture is important in 'remaking feminism' as they claim it is complicit rather than critical of capitalism.

Similarly, as Rottenberg (2014a) observes, confidence is sexy because it doesn't challenge 'the patriarchal gaze'. She maintains that its value is partly related to the fact that it is both attractive to men and requires no change on the part of men. Rottenberg calls the reformulation of feminism as 'neoliberal feminism', and she argues that the transformative nature of feminism is focused within women's psyches thus leaving the wider capitalist structures unchanged.

Another important dimension of the 'confidence culture' as identified by Gill and Orgad (2017) is favouring positivity over negativity. They argue that in preferring positive affect and outlawing negativity, the confidence culture dismisses more 'political' aspects of feeling, for example anger, indignation and complaint. The focus is on reworking them on an individual basis. Gill and Orgad maintain that this view combines the political, psychological and aesthetic. They claim that this is linked to a wider tendency within popular feminism to see feminism as an 'appealing and stylish identity' rather than a politically transformative movement.

The author has provided an analysis of the application of the 'confidence culture' to the novel *Big Little Lies* by the Australian novelist Liane Moriarty, and its serialization on HBO (see Brooks, 2022).

Gill and Orgad argue that ultimately the conclusion of their analysis of the 'confidence culture' for feminism is that it has transformed the political underpinnings of feminism. They maintain that their discussion of the confidence culture shows the neoliberalization and individualization of feminism and how it is involved in reformulating feminism. This includes: a reassessment of self by focusing on self-monitoring and the development of an 'entrepreneurial spirit' and a rejection of the structural conditions which ultimately produce inequality.

Rottenberg's (2014a) analysis offers a useful political critique of the impact of the transformation on feminism. She argues that the US is now dominated by neoliberal feminism, which she argues is captured in Sandberg's *Lean In* as well as in Anne-Marie Slaughter's work. She claims that neoliberal feminism offers no critique of neoliberalism and is in sync with neoliberalism. As Rottenberg (2014a: 420) comments: 'The neoliberal feminist subject is thus mobilized to convert continued gender inequality from a structural problem into an individual affair.'

Rottenberg, importantly, draws on the work of the outstanding feminist theorist Nancy Fraser (2013). Rottenberg (2014a: 421) provides a synopsis of Fraser's analysis. Fraser has been very critical of what she regards as the way in which dominant aspects of feminism have been complicit with neoliberal capitalism. In her article 'Feminism, capitalism, and the cunning of history', Fraser (2013) argues that second-wave feminism's privileging of recognition, as in identity, over redistribution (that is dealing with inequality) has resulted in feminism's convergence with neoliberal capitalism. Fraser is thus arguing that the claim that feminism is merging with neoliberalism is the result of second-wave feminism's failure to align itself with a materialist critique.

Fraser's (2013) critique of second-wave feminism is based on the fact that it has 'forfeit[ed] the demand for economic redistribution' [which] ended up serving as a key enabler for 'the new spirit of neoliberalism' (Fraser, 2013: 220). Rottenberg (2014a) addresses the issue of feminism's intersection with neoliberalism, which she argues produces a new kind of feminist subject. Rottenberg maintains that while she doesn't agree with Fraser's critique, she argues that Fraser's work reinforces the emergence of a new form of feminism which is defined by market rationality.

In a powerful indictment of what she regards as the transformation of feminism, Rottenberg (2014a: 432) claims that the rise of neoliberal feminism is the result of multiple sources. She argues that as more White, middle-class women remain in the public sphere even after they have had children, this new form of feminist discourse tends to offset the critique from other strands of feminism. She argues that the focus on neoliberal feminism tends to diminish other issues which have always been important to feminism, including the gendered wage gap, sexual harassment, rape or domestic violence, and she maintains that it positions ambitious, individual, middle-class women as part of the problem, yet also part of the solution within neoliberal feminism.

Building on Rottenberg's analysis, Gill and Kanai (2018), in 'Mediating neoliberal capitalism: affect, subjectivity and inequality', discuss the links between neoliberalism and the 'commercialization of feeling', or what Illouz (2007) describes as a new era of 'emotional capitalism'. Illouz argues that this is generating new 'structures of feeling'. They also make the case for expanding the theoretical and conceptual vocabulary in order to foreground the relationship between neoliberalism, media and subjectivity.

## In summary

Chapter 5 has reviewed how emotions intersect with class. The chapter initially showed how traditional conceptions of emotional capital related to the work of Bourdieu (1984) and how it is important in understanding later conceptions of cultural capital. The role of gender in its intersection with class was reviewed in the work of some of the second-wave feminist theorists, including Storr (2002), Reay (2004) and Skeggs (2010). The chapter looked at how this work is built on through the analysis of emotions, consumption and commodities, as developed in the work of a number of feminist and cultural theorists, in particular Illouz (1997a, 2009, 2018). Finally, the chapter showed that contemporary feminists have further developed the analysis to explore the intersection of emotion, neoliberalism and consumption, particularly examining the 'confidence culture'.

6

# Positive and Negative Emotions

## Introduction

Chapter 6 examines positive and negative emotions. A distinction is made between positive and negative emotions in the Introduction. Positive emotions have been associated with 'happiness studies' and the theorization of happiness has been of interest to a wide range of theorists, from Jeremy Bentham (1789) to Sara Ahmed (2004, 2010). Part I of the chapter examines these theories as well as empirical research in the area of happiness. While Ahmed has theorized the area of happiness, she is also one of the key theorists who has investigated how a range of negative emotions, including anger and wretchedness, are linked to migration. In particular, Ahmed (2010), in 'Melancholic migrants' in *The Promise of Happiness*, shows how emotion is central within the social and political framework of understanding 'the stranger':

> To recognise somebody as a stranger is an affective judgement: a stranger is the one who seems suspicious; the one who lurks. I became interested in how some bodies are 'in an instant' judged as suspicious, or as dangerous, as objects to be feared, a judgement that can have lethal consequences. There can be nothing more dangerous to a body than the social arrangement that that body is dangerous. (Ahmed, 2010: 211)

Part II of the chapter focuses on negative emotions, specifically anger and shame, and examines how both concepts are explored by a number of significant theorists. Part III of the chapter explores the relationship between emotions, politics and war, and Part IV of the chapter explores emotions in the area of social abjection and how it relates to broader areas of social justice.

## Part I. Critical perspectives on happiness studies

It has been noteworthy that the late 20th century and early 21st century have been characterized by a rapid growth in happiness studies which have largely been driven by the growth of 'sub-disciplines' including 'positive psychology' and 'happiness economics'. Substantial social and cultural theorists such as Ahmed (2004, 2010) have also focused on the issue of happiness and Ahmed (2010) even talks about 'the turn to happiness'.

Some theorists see the emphasis on happiness as fulfilling the promise of the Enlightenment. Bruckner (2000) argues that the promise of the Enlightenment was of a 'messianic dawn' transforming 'tears' into 'roses'. The promise was of long-term fulfilment and happiness which was offered by 'scientific experts' and made available to a wide public in forms which were both accessible and digestible as popular literature. Bruckner (2000) maintains that this can be seen as fulfilling the Enlightenment project.

By contrast, Adorno (2005 [1951]: 62–3) argues that what he calls 'the gospel of happiness' is in reality a technique of domination which is espoused by psychologists, psychiatrists and the entertainment industry to dull the senses and distract from suffering.

The discovery of 'the science of happiness' is of course linked to the bizarre set of concepts and language emanating from the psy-sciences and the idea of 'the therapeutic turn' providing a psychological crutch and creating the 'mental health industry' which dominated the latter part of the 20th and early 21st centuries. As Hill et al (2019: 3) note, the psy-sciences in the form of psychology, psychiatry and to a lesser extent medicine have generated an entire 'self-help' vocabulary around emotion, desire, pathology and despair.

The history of the science of happiness has its roots in the utilitarian movement and the work of Jeremy Bentham (1969 [1789]). Bentham asserted that 'human conduct is governed by two sovereign masters: the pursuit of pleasure and the avoidance of pain' (cited in Hill et al, 2019: 5). Bentham wanted to develop scientific tools to measure happiness but he was unsuccessful, and the issue of how happiness was measured remained limited up to the second half of the 20th century (to be discussed later).

Hill et al (2019: 7) maintain that the happiness industry as promoted by Davies (2015) among others is littered with psy-scientists, including psychologists, psychiatrists and a range of therapeutically inspired actors, as well as 'economists, self-help practitioners, New Age gurus, and self-styled life coaches'. It is claimed that scientific discourses of happiness have been adopted in popular culture and widely promoted by a range of theorists and writers including Illouz (2008), Wright (2011) and Hsu and Madsen (2019). Happiness by this group is seen as central to mental and physical well-being and promoted as an asset.

Regardless of this emphasis, and the fact that there are improvements in life expectancy, living standards and the quality of life, people are not as happy as might be expected (Ahmed, 2010). Davies (2015) argues that there is a pervasive nervousness in social life which could be the result of ongoing crises, including climate change, financial crisis and terrorism. Davies includes the rise of populism, including Brexit and the rise of Trump.

Turner (2018) claims that the modern secular regime of happiness is linked to two powerful narratives that attempt to explain the relationship between modernity and happiness. The first narrative is that happiness is viewed as a promise of the Enlightenment's emphasis on rationality. The second narrative says that modernity is viewed as a 'disorienting and disturbing loss of meaning and purpose' (2018).

However, as Hill et al (2019: 9) comment, capitalism has been able to 'absorb critique and put it to work for its own ends resulting in what Boltanski and Chiapello (2007) term "a new spirit of capitalism"'. As Turner (2018) observes: 'The appeal of happiness is that it grapples with two dominant narratives that detail the effect of modernity: happiness as crisis and happiness as promise' (cited in Hill et al, 2019: 10).

In terms of the measurement of happiness, perhaps the most famous has been the development of the gross national happiness (GNH) index by the King of Bhutan in 1972. The story is an interesting one. King Jigme Singye Wangchuck of Bhutan was very concerned that the social changes he wanted to make after the opening of the kingdom to capitalism had not been well received. Thus he suggested an alternative measure of progress, which was gross national happiness (GNH), claiming that it was more important than gross national product (GNP). The Kingdom of Bhutan offered GNH as an alternative measure of societal progress through the UN in the 1990s, which led to the establishment of *World Happiness Day* and an annual publication, the *World Happiness Report* (Helliwell et al, 2019).

Duncan (2019: 84) maintains that 'a world ranking of happiness surveys should place Norway, Denmark and Iceland at the top and at the bottom, Tanzania, Burundi and Central African Republic (Helliwell et al, 2019)' (cited in Duncan, 2019: 84). As Duncan comments, the most effective way for social researchers to consider measuring happiness is to consider statistical evidence 'that suggests that social belonging, social rights and good democratic governance correlate positively with the mean self-reported happiness scores of a population (Bok, 2010; Dutt and Radcliff, 2009; Frey and Stutzer, 2009)' (Duncan, 2019: 86).

Duncan also indicates that David Cameron argued that UK official statistics should include indicators of social well-being, and the outputs of public reports now advise governments on the primacy of happiness as a goal. However, as Duncan notes, regardless of global bodies developing sets of social indicators, the 'universal ideal of happiness masks political ideology' (Duncan, 2019: 88).

In an article entitled 'Hijacking the language of functionality? In praise of "negative emotions against happiness"', Cabanas and Illouz (2019: 67) contextualize the role of happiness in neoliberal society. They argue that happiness has become the pervasive ideology in neoliberal societies. In an interesting historical trajectory of such emotion-related movements, it is claimed that following developments such as therapeutic culture (Nolan, 1998), emotional capitalism (Illouz, 2007, 2008), and neo-utilitarian politics (Lamont, 2012) and the 'self-help transnational industry (Nehring et al, 2016)', the emergence of positive psychology today is in the forefront of what is called an 'epidemic' of developments that has defined a range of societal dimensions covering 'mortality, politics, economics and therapeutics'.

Cabanas and Illouz note that happiness scientists have established a positive emotional narrative that posits a clear divide between normal/abnormal, healthy/hazardous, desirable/undesirable and functional/dysfunctional. They also note that 'positive psychology's' approach to emotions, which is essentially a conformist political ideology, 'overlooks the tight relationship of emotions to changing patterns of choice and consumption (e.g. Illouz, 2007, 2008, 2012, 2018), as well as social structures – that is social situations and power relations (e.g. Barbalet, 2004; Hochschild, 2012)' (Cabanas and Illouz, 2019: 73).

They also make the interesting point that the idea that positive and negative emotions produce positive and negative outcomes respectively is oversimplistic. Cabanas and Illouz (2019: 73) give a couple of interesting examples in showing that 'joyfulness' encourages individuals to engage in challenging activities, but to possibly be less resilient when faced with difficult tasks or even to make less accurate choices, and to encourage conformity and acquiescence (Tan and Forgas, 2010; Forgas, 2013). On the other hand, 'forgiveness' could reduce hostility towards others, but it could also in some circumstances produce the opposite effect; for example, forgiveness may be a benefit for couples who rarely engage in arguments but could be detrimental to those who fight regularly (Perez-Alvarez, 2012).

In their collection *Dystopian Emotions*, McKenzie and Patulny (2022: 5) argue that the new era of politics has made the concept of dystopia a mainstream phenomenon. They make the point that '… there is an ambivalent contradiction in the experience of hope and pessimism in contemporary views of the future.' Bauman's *Modernity and Ambivalence* (1993) shows that an 'overly rationalised modernity' could not make sense of the disorderly reality which characterized it. In addition, Burkitt (1997) extends the concept of 'dystopia' to the work of Norbert Elias and more broadly the concept of civilization.

Beyond the theoretical sophistication, McKenzie and Patulny also show how utopian and dystopian language can be seen in a range of social movements: 'Examples such as the Occupy Movement, Black Lives Matter, #Me Too and Extinction Rebellion, all engage with and can draw from aspects of utopia and dystopia. … In each of these movements, dystopian and apocalyptic realities inspire collective micro-utopian praxis as well as macro-scale planning for alternative futures' (McKenzie and Patulny, 2022: 7).

McKenzie and Patulny also show how this emotional ambivalence and anxiety was prevalent among classical theorists. These theorists reflected the collective angst of the times. As has been noted elsewhere, Weber predicted a period of *disenchantment* of the world as outlined by Taylor (2007). In the case of Simmel's ([1903] 2004) concept of the *Blasé Attitude* (or Outlook), this refers to what is defined as the diminished emotional engagement which Simmel argues is needed to survive in modern dense cities. Weber and Simmel are both mourning the loss of something meaningful and are not endorsing this way of living. Both of these classical sociological theorists are dealing with the de-emotionalization of modern society and individuals and also hint at what they see as the darkness of modernity as a cold and inhuman environment.

The classical theorists were not the only theorists interested in the emotional impact of change. McKenzie and Patulny (2022: 10) show how Bauman (1991) was also preoccupied with similar debates on the emotional consequences of postmodernity. They show that in *Modernity and Ambivalence*, Bauman (1991) proposes a theory of rationalization. Bauman maintains that in a rational world, individuals are left without the skills needed to navigate disorder; this results in detachment from the world and de-emotionalization.

In their conclusion, McKenzie and Patulny (2022) consider some of the dimensions of emotions which have complicated the picture. The first of these is the impact of specific emotions; Patulny and McKenzie give examples of anger in US politics (Hochschild, 2016) and distress over climate change (Albrecht et al, 2007).

A further dimension is the role of affect which has been the focus of some of the early theorists (Ahmed, 2004). They argue that this provides focus for the 'underlying emotional dynamics, cultures and climates (de Riviera, 1992)' of different societies. McKenzie and Patulny (2022: 177) look at the impact of COVID-19 on emotions, and much of the research has yet to be undertaken. COVID-19 has generated extensive research and a wide range of responses and has instigated a rise in fear over concerns with health, employment and social cohesion. It has been argued that much of the COVID-19 fears and anxiety has built on pre-existing fears over areas such as health, employment and politics. Examples of these areas include Beck's (1992) analysis of risk societies, Bauman's (2005) analysis of liquid modernity, Sennett's (1998) analysis of social drift and Habermas's (1990) focus on the decline of the public sphere.

Loneliness is another area which has become an important focal point for research in late modernity, as shown in the work of Franklin et al (2019), Hookway et al (2019) and Patulny and Olson (2019). This is partly the result of the transitionary and fluid nature of relationships, as shown by Giddens (1991) and Bauman (2005), and the decline of coupled households and increase in single-person dwellings, as shown by Qu (2020) (see McKenzie and Patulny, 2022).

Happiness is one of the most researched concepts, as already noted, and one of the most significant theorists of happiness has been Sara Ahmed (2007, 2008). In 'Multiculturalism and the promise of happiness', Ahmed (2007) claims that the new science of happiness might uncouple happiness from the accumulation of wealth, but still locates happiness in areas such as marriage. However, she notes that the 'happy housewife' has largely been replaced by a 'desperate' one as there has been a shift in how happiness is defined within marriage.

Perhaps more interestingly, she cites the work of American journalist Meghan O'Rourke in her article 'Desperate feminist wives', where she draws on a study of happiness in the US which suggests that feminist women are less happy than 'traditional housewives'. In fact, as Ahmed notes, marriage is still widely regarded as the primary 'happiness indicator'.

Elsewhere, Ahmed (2008), in her article 'The happiness turn', makes the point that the turn to happiness is related to therapeutic cultures and discourses of self-help, and as noted earlier is linked to the subfield of positive psychology. She makes the point that 'the happiness industry' is both produced and consumed through these self-help books, which can be seen as 'accumulating value as a form of capital'.' As noted, happiness levels are linked to 'happiness indicators', with marriage seen as an important happiness indicator.

Happiness is not a neutral phenomenon, but linked to social norms. Berlant (2004) regards this 'fantasy of happiness' as a stupid form of optimism, as she comments: 'the faith that adjustment to certain forms or practices of living and thinking will secure one's happiness' (Berlant, 2004: 75) (cited in Ahmed, 2008: 10). Ahmed (2008: 12) notes that 'Berlant (2007b) considers the affective range of optimism, and how optimism involves "a cluster of promises" … Optimism for Berlant can be cruel (though not always …) and has an intimate relation of how subjects endure situations of poverty, violence and despair.'

Ahmed also draws on Love (2007) who

> addresses the promissory logic of happiness by considering the idealisation of marriage. Love considers the significance of queer unhappiness in *Brokeback Mountain* [film], asking whether queer politics should invest its hopes and longings in the image of the good life implicit in marriage, or even the 'happy ending' of coupledom, or whether the task for queers might be to find joy and pleasure elsewhere. … (Ahmed, 2008: 12)

The key issue for most of the work around happiness is that it tends to be focused on heterosexual relationships, as is the concept of affect, and this creates a limited understanding of both happiness and love more broadly.

## Part II. Other emotions – anger and shame

Apart from happiness, a number of other emotions have elicited interesting responses from theorists, including anger and shame. Henderson (2008), in focusing on anger, makes the important point that emotions need to be understood in a politically meaningful way, and she also shows how a historical perspective is also important. She traces the historiography of anger.

Henderson challenges the idea that anger necessarily leads to negative socio-political outcomes and should be avoided. She argues that this is similar to the stand taken on shame, which Probyn (2004: 329, 346) maintains is 'immensely productive politically and conceptually in advancing a project of everyday ethics ...', even though 'not all uses of shame are good'. Henderson distinguishes between shame and anger and whether they should be considered an emotion or an affect and focuses on the former. She raises the question of how we make sense of emotions in a politically meaningful way. She argues that the critical challenge to this view suggests that 'it is too masculinist, too mechanistic and too far removed from the lived experiences of an emotional (human) subject (Thien, 2005)' (Henderson, 2008: 29).

The second reason identified by Henderson in defence of anger 'is because it can locate blame for injustice, and tends more than other emotions, to motivate punitive and or preventative demands against the unjust treatment of others' (Henderson, 2008: 30). She looks at transgressions of feeling rules and how they are met with sanctions. Henderson argues that the sanctions employed are interpreted by feminist scholars as a refusal to acknowledge the expression of emotions, in other words, a refusal to recognize the legitimacy of particular emotions. She gives anger as an example and argues that anger as an emotion is often dismissed when applied to women, and to a range of different minority groups including 'visible minorities, aboriginal, the working-class, the disabled, the ill, the divorced and the old as bitterness ...' (Henderson, 2008: 30).

Henderson, drawing on the work of Stearns and Stearns (1986), argues that an understanding of changes in anger and other emotions may be one of the central linkages between personal and public spheres, and that anger is connected to political behaviour. Henderson (2008: 33) also shows that there is a strong class dimension in the expression of anger and notes that written accounts of anger from the 13th to the early 16th centuries suggest that anger in this period was 'essentially a noble prerogative' (Freedman, 1998: 171), and that it was linked to honour and was considered out of place in the lower classes and in peasants.

Henderson's (2008) work is particularly interesting in her use of socio-historical research. Apart from drawing on European historical references, Henderson also draws on historical material from the US. She shows that US publications dating from the mid-18th century show a significant tendency towards 'promoting an anger-free home as a refuge from the risk and fatigue of factory life' (Henderson, 2008: 33).

The early part of this period emphasized a sense of domestic idealism, where anger should be entirely 'exorcised' from the family sphere. However, as the century moved to its end, this idealism became more relaxed. Societal views of anger changed, and while it was still frowned upon in the home, it became viewed as a more 'natural' emotion which couldn't be entirely repressed, but which could be, as Stearns and Stearns (1986) maintain, channelled more productively into the public sphere.

Another concept which has attracted theoretical and conceptual interest is 'shame'. Elspeth Probyn (2004), in 'Everyday shame', draws on and extends Bourdieu's notion of 'habitus', and argues for the positivity of everyday shame. Probyn's work politicizes the concept of shame in the context of a postcolonial milieu and draws on an Australian context to develop her position. Probyn (2004) comments as follows:

> Shame is the body's way of registering that it has been interested, and that it seeks to re-establish interest … Here I explore shame and interest as resources in rethinking concepts such as the everyday habitus … Shame also provides a way of navigating the complexity of everyday life in a postcolonial milieu … (Probyn, 2004: 329)

Probyn draws on Aboriginal and non-Aboriginal cultures to illustrate the point and argues: 'I want to argue that shame is immensely productive politically and conceptually in advancing a project of everyday ethics' (Probyn, 2004: 329). From a theoretical perspective, Probyn develops how shame is seen and whether it is understood as an affect or an emotion.

Probyn (2004: 330) argues that descriptions of shame tend to be differentiated according to whether it is seen as an affect or an emotion. In general, she argues that descriptions of shame which are defined as an emotion tend to focus on knowledge and intellect and even disparage shame related to the body. By comparison, in defining shame in terms of affect, theorists are more open to explaining shame in relation to the body.

## Part III. Emotions, politics and trauma

The sociology of emotions has also been developed in the context of politics, trauma and war. Ahall and Gregory (2015) examine the intersection of emotions, politics and war, and in doing so they draw on a number of theorists including Berlant (2004) and Ahmed (2004).

In the case of Berlant (2004), she has 'focused her attention on the *effects* of compassion in producing and maintaining exclusionary practices. The emphasis of compassion, she argues, is not on the experiences of those who are suffering, but on the experiences of those watching from afar (Berlant, 2004: 1–2; Sedgwick, 2003)' (cited in Ahall and Gregory, 2015: 4).

In addition, Ahmed (2004), in *The Cultural Politics of Emotion*, uses emotions more broadly within the context of 'impression' which is an attempt to avoid making analytical distinctions between bodily sensations and more cognitive impact, as though they could be experienced as distinct realms of human 'experience' (see Ahmed, 2004).

Ahmed makes the point that emotions are not simply feelings related to an individual but are cultural constructs. In an interesting example of this, she uses 'hate' as an emotion to develop the point. She argues that we should not understand 'hate' as an expression of something innate, such as an innate dislike that is buried deep within an individual psyche. Rather, Ahmed argues that the development of hate is a result of past encounters and associations which have resulted in certain groups being demarcated as posing a threat to a particular way of life (Ahmed, 2004). This can be seen in the response to refugees/migrants which have become a feature of the British response to the influx of migrants on small boats from France. This response is amplified by the Conservative government's response to 'Stop the boats' in July 2023. In this case it can be seen as an emotional response exacerbated by a political response.

Ahall and Gregory (2015) consider research undertaken on politics, emotions and war and make the point that much of the work has approached 'emotions' through 'feelings, predominantly negatively'. They argue that a lot of this work can be traced back to the terrorist attacks in the US, in particular the September 11, 2001 terrorist attacks and the ensuing 'war on terror'.

Hutchinson (2010: 66), in her work on the constitution of identity, security and community after the Bali bombing in 2002, focuses on trauma. Hutchinson argues that trauma is often viewed as experience that isolates individuals and undermines a sense of community and she maintains that the narratives often used to make sense of a traumatic event can help produce a sense of community and togetherness. This can be clearly seen in the tragic fires on the Hawaiian island of Maui in August 2023, and the way in which the community pulled together in the face of the complete devastation of the town of Lahaina and the loss of 150 people.

Jeffrey Alexander (2012), in *Trauma: A Social Theory*, is concerned with collective traumas. He makes the distinction between individual victims of trauma and collectivities as follows:

> *Individual* victims react to traumatic injury with repression and denial, gaining relief when these psychological defences are overcome, bringing pain into consciousness so they are able to mourn. For *collectivities,* it is different. Rather than denial, repression and 'working through', it is a matter of symbolic construction and framing, of creating stories and characters, and moving along from there. (Alexander, 2012: 3)

Alexander (2012) describes 'cultural trauma' as follows; he says that for traumas to emerge at the level of the collectivity, social crises must become cultural crises. The fires on Maui are a clear example of this. Alexander (2012) argues that cultural traumas occur when members of a collectivity experience a horrendous and shocking event which leaves an indelible mark upon the group consciousness, thereby, as Alexander (2012: 6) notes, 'marking their memories forever and changing their future identity in fundamental and irrelevant ways'. Alexander argues that experiencing trauma can be understood as a sociological process, which can be defined as an injury to the collectivity. This, he maintains, creates a victim, attributes responsibility and distributes both 'the ideal and material consequences' (Alexander, 2012: 26).

Elsewhere, Ahall and Gregory (2013) draw on the work of Judith Butler (2004). Butler shows that within the politics of grief, it is possible to delineate between lives which she describes as 'grievable' and those that are not. She argues that non-Western lives have become 'unmarkable' within what are defined as the dominant frames of war, which are defined by racial violence which has made their lives 'unintelligible'.

## Part IV. Social abjection

In her book *Revolting Subjects: Social Abjection and Resistance in Neoliberal Britain*, Tyler (2013) draws on Kristeva's (1982) psychoanalytic account of abjection but argues for a more fully social and political account of abjection through a consideration of the consequences of '"being abject" within specific social and political locales' (Tyler, 2013: 4). In this she identifies a number of 'disenfranchised populations', including migrants in detention and facing deportation, the position of Gypsies and Travellers and the riots of young people in the summer of 2011 among others. Tyler's work is original and despite drawing on Kristeva's work is significantly sociological and contemporary in recognizing a wide range of marginalized communities. This is an important area for the sociology of emotions, as shown earlier, and surfaces important dimensions of social inequality and social power.

In conceptualizing and theorizing this area, Tyler (2013: 22) draws on the concept of 'disgust' and recognizes that the concept was once a neglected area of scholarship. However, she notes that over the past 20 years there has been a significant body of research focusing on 'disgust', as well as other 'aversive' emotions, which Tyler argues are examples of 'ugly feelings' and their social and political function. She cites the work of a number of important feminist and other theorists in this regard, including Probyn (2000), Meagher (2003), Menninghaus (2003), Ahmed (2004), Nussbaum (2004) and Ngai (2005). Drawing on Nussbaum (2004: 107), Tyler argues that 'disgust' has been used throughout history 'as a powerful weapon in social efforts to exclude certain groups and persons.'

Tyler's work is important in injecting a political dimension to the analysis of emotions. Her objective in undertaking this analysis is to show how neoliberalism (Harvey, 2005) produces groups of people who are the subject of negative emotions. Tyler (2013) has deliberately drawn on a wide range of different categories and groups of people, which she argues are 'laid to waste' by economic, political and social policies related to neoliberalism. She gives a number of examples of such marginalized groups, including asylum seekers and other 'unwanted irregular' migrants, politically and economically disenfranchised young people, Gypsies and Travellers and people with disabilities. Tyler argues that her aim is to develop an intersectional account of marginalization and that this will deepen an understanding of the processes involved in 'neoliberal governmentality' (Tyler, 2013: 8).

## In summary

This chapter has explored the diverse field of positive and negative conceptual frameworks and theories on the emotions, examining a range of theorists from cultural studies, feminist and sociological perspectives. The chapter opened with a critical analysis of happiness studies which has been the focus for a number of theorists. Part II of the chapter explored a number of other concepts, including anger and shame. Part III of the chapter examined how emotions intersect with issues of politics, trauma and war, which included exploring the issue of individual and collective trauma. Part IV examined the issue of social abjection from a sociological perspective and how it relates to broader issues of social justice.

7

# Emotions, Love and Intimacy

## Introduction

Chapter 7 reviews the relationship of emotion, love and intimacy and looks at some of the key contributors to this growing field, which includes theoretical perspectives on traditional and contemporary models of love and intimacy. The chapter draws on perspectives from feminist, sociological and cultural theorists who have offered a wide range of theoretical and conceptual frameworks in understanding the relationship between love, intimacy and emotions. The chapter adopts a socio-historical perspective in analyzing the work of writers and theorists in the field, including Giddens (1991, 1992); Beck and Beck-Gernsheim ([1995] 2002); Illouz (1997a, 1998, 2010, 2012); Shumway (2003); Gross (2005) and O'Neill (2015a, 2015b), as well as the author's earlier work in the field (Brooks, 2017, 2019a). The chapter is divided into three sections as follows: Part I. Romantic love and the emergence of intimacy; Part II. Romance as a postmodern condition: Illouz, love and the cultural contradictions of capitalism; Part III. 'Mediated intimacy' in heterosexual men.

## Part I. Romantic love and the emergence of intimacy

Shumway offers an important socio-historical contextualization of the field of romantic love and the growth of intimacy. Love and marriage is of course at its heart an economic and class-based enterprise. As Shumway (2003: 7) shows: 'The aristocrats needed marriages of alliance to preserve their power and wealth, and the working class typically married for the economic advantages that extra hands brought to the household.'

Gross (2005) makes the important point that narratives of romantic love have their origins in the West. Gross argues that the origins of romantic love are very clearly Western, and not, as is sometimes thought, universal. Their origins are in narratives of courtly love which first emerged in verse in the 11th and 12th centuries in Aquitaine and Provence (see Bloch, 1992; Duby, 1994).

Gross notes that the term 'courtly love' was first used in 1883, when Gaston Paris, the French medievalist, used it to describe the passionate love which characterized the love between Lancelot and Guinevere in Chrétien de Troyes's 12th-century romantic verse in Old French entitled *Lancelot ou le chevalier de la charette*. The basis of these romantic narratives were romantic liaisons in which knights in the royal courts proclaimed their love for and fell in love with married noblewomen. This may have resulted in these women becoming involved in extra-marital affairs, although whether they were sexually consummated is unclear.

The important dimension of this romantic love narrative is that both love and its 'object of desire' were 'idealized and sacralized'. This elevated the romantic love narrative into a different sphere and created a narrative which has become a significant part of the historical development of romantic love. Gross also makes the important point that romantic love was not something that could arise within marriage. In this regard, Shumway (2003: 14) draws on 'Andreas Capellanus's twelfth century treatise, *The Art of Courtly Love*' which claims that '[e]verybody knows that love can have no place between husband and wife'.

Shumway is one of the best writers in the field in his socio-historical exposition of romantic love. Shumway shows that romance emerged as a counter discourse which represented an alternative to the 'repressive character of officially sanctioned marriage among the aristocracy' (Shumway, 2003: 13).

Gross argues that during the 18th and 19th centuries, this socio-historical model of romantic love was challenged and recast in the West to apply to marital law. Gross notes that the concept of erotic or passionate love was not unheard of before the 18th century, but the general assumption was that love did not form the basis of marriage (see Gross, 2005).

Shumway (2003) argues that it was only in the 19th century that marriage began to be associated with romance. But he points out that this didn't mean that marriage suddenly became more passionate or loving. In fact, the nature of Victorian sexual repression resulted in men continuing to seek sexual satisfaction outside marriage. Shumway shows that love within marriage was often associated with friendship rather than romance and pleasure. He maintains that conceptions of love and marriage in the 19th century were divided among an emphasis on companionate marriage, on those deriving from romance and those drawing on traditional social and economic factors.

He also shows that the interrelationship of romance and marriage was probably more clearly defined in America than elsewhere in the late 19th and 20th centuries, and this was reinforced in print and on screen. He cites the work of Frances Cancian (1987), whose book *Love in America: Gender and Self-Development* sets out what marital intimacy in America might have looked like: 'marital intimacy in the modern sense of emotional expression and verbal disclosure of personal experience, was probably rare. Instead, husband and wife were likely to share a more formal and wordless kind of love, based on duty, working together, mutual help, and sex' (Cancian, 1987: 17, cited in Shumway, 2003: 24).

More broadly, Gross (2005) shows that in the 19th century romance frequently involved 'self-revelation', however, as romance has evolved through the 20th century, under the influence of a variety of 'therapeutic discourses', romance has seemingly been reframed as a process of revealing all one's psychological vulnerabilities and life experiences. The dominance of the psy-sciences as shown in earlier chapters have resulted in changes to romantic love narratives. The focus has shifted from what were previously seen as obligations to family and society, to a capacity to work through psychological barriers to intimacy (see Swidler, 2001).

In this vein, Hazleden (2004) draws on contemporary relationship manuals to highlight the focus on issues of reflexivity in recent theoretical debates. Some of the most profound theoretical developments in sociology have revolved around a focus on the growth of individualization in late modernity. As Gross (2005) indicates, some social theorists focus on the individualized nature of intimacy today, such as Giddens (1991, 1992) and Beck and Beck-Gernsheim (2002), or how intimacy is structured through its encounters with late capitalism, as shown in the work of Lasch (1977), Illouz (1997a), Hochschild (2003) and Kipnis (2003). Others, such as Bauman (2000), have analyzed the relationship between intimacy and postmodernity.

Hazleden (2004) and others maintain that Giddens (1991, 1992) is central in understanding the transformation of intimacy. Giddens (1992) has put forward the idea of 'therapeutic culture' which has emerged alongside reflexivity. He maintains that late modernity has seen the rise of the 'pure relationship' and 'confluent love', which he argues has been generated largely by women. He claims that these phenomena are liberatory and goes on to say that it might lead to a 'reconciliation of the sexes'.

Giddens makes comparisons between relationship manuals as social and cultural indicators and medieval manuals of manners that Norbert Elias investigated (see earlier chapters). As Hazleden (2004: 202) comments: 'seeing relationship manuals as expressive of processes of reflexivity, which they chart out and help shape', he [Giddens] views such texts as an important part of this 'reconciliation of the sexes'. However, Giddens claims that self-help books are able to empower individuals and not challenge relationships of power.

While Giddens (1991, 1992) and Beck and Beck-Gernsheim (2002) are often discussed as sharing the same theoretical position, they do differ. Gross (2005) outlines the similarities and differences in their positions. Beck and Beck-Gernsheim (2002) share with Giddens an interest in 'pure relationships'. However, they maintain that the emphasis on 'flexibility, negotiation, and contingency' in intimate relationships is not a result of the influence of globalization (as Giddens maintains), but is the result of the process of individualization which has taken place in late modernity. Beck and Beck-Gernsheim (2002) argue that while individualization was an important concept in classical versions of modernization theory, they claim that the individual in late modernity is different from the individual in modernity.

Not all social theorists agree with Giddens. Jamieson (1999: 265) has famously criticized Giddens, by launching an incisive critique which 'juxtaposes Giddens's theoretical claims of sexual democracy with the lived realities of unequal gender relations'. She argues that there is a significant tension in attempting to sustain relationships characterized by intimacy and openness required by the ideal of a 'pure relationship', while at the same time setting this in the context of the structural framework of gender inequalities. This results in couples developing a 'shared repertoire of cover stories, taboos and self-dishonesty' (Jamieson, 1999: 265) which are framed around 'asymmetries in parenting, domestic labour and "emotion work" (Brannen and Moss, 1991; Hochschild, 1994)' (Jamieson, 1999: 265).

Hochschild (1994) maintains there is what she calls 'a cultural cooling' in relation to intimate life in her study of advice books published between 1970 and 1990. She identifies a shift from female to male 'rules of love' – in other words, she argues that late modernity is characterized by a culture which defines personal relationships that 'seek to re-cycle male feeling rules to women' (Hochschild, 1994: 28 n 3). Hochschild sees this is as part of a 'hi-jacking' of feminism by both capitalist and instrumentalist values which she argues were both separate from and alien to feminism (see Hazleden, 2004).

Gross (2005: 301) adds to the debate in the discussion on the 'detraditionalization of intimacy' and argues that for a number of theorists, the 'detraditionalization of intimacy' means the feelings traditionally associated with narratives of romantic love have been displaced; these include warmth, comfort and closeness.

They maintain that intimate bonds have a superficial and contingent quality which Gross argues reflect an 'unrivalled hegemony of market logics', as well as the decline of traditions where the emphasis is on the importance of lifetime commitments which created a sense of enchantment around intimacy. Gross claims that Hochschild (2003) epitomizes this position with her analysis of 'cool modern love'.

However, Gross (2005: 301) also shows that other theorists, including Beck and Beck-Gernsheim (2002), while they may support the detraditionalization position, take an opposing view and argue that narratives of romantic love, including the experiences to which they give meaning, are a feature of the intimacy landscape at a time when they are seen as needed in a fragmented and anomic world. Gross also indicates that for Americans who attend college, romance remains very important, and he comments that we may have entered a time where 'hook-ups' become more common than dating. This issue is further explored by Shumway (2022).

## Part II. Romance as a postmodern condition: Illouz, love and the cultural contradictions of capitalism

Eva Illouz (1997a, 1998, 2010, 2012) is one of the most interesting theorists in the field, and successfully combines theoretical and conceptual dimensions in her analysis. She succeeds over others in the field of love and intimacy in continually amplifying her analysis to accommodate external developments and brings together sociological and feminist theory with cultural theory. The author reviews some but not all her work and further analysis of her work can be found in Brooks (2017, 2019).

Turner (1998) reviews Illouz's (1997a) *Consuming the Romantic Utopia: Love and the Cultural Contradictions of Capitalism*. He argues that Illouz's study of the 'romanticization of commodities' and the 'commodification of romance' is important in developing the tradition of the genre both conceptually and theoretically. However, Turner notes that her sociology of romance is very distinctive for two reasons. In the first instance, because it has its traditions in the 'analysis of qualitative empirical data'. Secondly, it focuses on the 'actual "practice" of love rather than ideas about it' (Turner, 1998: 115). The author would add a third element, in that Illouz's work is grounded in real world experiences and is important in bringing together theoretical and empirical dimensions.

Much of Illouz's work has been concerned to understand the transformation of love in the 20th and 21st centuries though the association of love and consumerism, but her analysis also includes a common-sense view of class in the socio-historical evolution of love and intimacy. Illouz (1997a) claims that intimacy as an ideal is an important historically positioned form of wellbeing, and she cites a number of writers and theorists in this regard, including Cancian (1987), Stone (1997), and Beck and Beck-Gernsheim (2002).

She argues that romantic love has been an aspect of the rise of the educated middle class and can be seen as an important part of the 'bourgeois ideal of private life' (Illouz, 1997a: 54). Further, Illouz argues that the growth of capitalism and the liberal state have broken down the connections between family and 'associative life', which she maintains prevailed up to the 19th century. 'Associative life' is derived from the French term '*vie associative*' and acts as a mediator between individuals and the state. In addition, she argues that as the individual's biography has become defined by both the state and the market, the family, and a more abstract ideal of intimacy, have become more prominent in the definition of modern identity. This, she argues, is represented in the work of Giddens (1992) as well as Beck and Beck-Gernsheim ([1995] 2002).

Elsewhere, Illouz (1998) follows the tradition of romantic love, drawing on Lawrence Stone (1997) and Niklas Luhmann (1986) on cultural expectations of love. She focuses on the concept of 'love at first sight' and shows that it was not until the end of the 18th century that the concept of 'infatuation' became more prominent and became defined, as Illouz describes it, 'as being foolishly in love'. She argues that there are two distinct narratives, one of sex (infatuation) and one of love. Thus, on the one hand, sexuality was integrated with love, whereas on the other hand there were medical and political discourses which she said 'disentangled' sex from emotions it was supposed to express.

Thus Illouz argues that sexuality was legitimated for its own sake and, in addition, it 'demystifies' the narrative of 'love at first sight' on the grounds that it was essentially about sexual attraction. Illouz maintains therefore that in the Romantic tradition, sex and sexual arousal was legitimated as 'love at first sight'. By contrast, in contemporary society, the idea of love at first sight is largely seen as a pretence for what in reality is lust or sexual desire.

In contrast to the idea of 'love at first sight', Illouz shows how the growth of the postmodern romantic condition presents a very different model of romantic love to earlier models. The concept of 'subsuming the romantic biography under a single life-long narrative of love ("*le grand amour*")' (Illouz, 1998: 175) is contested by romance under postmodernism, as Illouz shows: 'postmodern romance has seen the collapse of overarching, life-long romantic narratives, which it has compressed into the briefer and repeatable form of the affair' (Illouz, 1998: 175).

One of the reasons for the emergence of this narrative is related to the transformation of sex and sexuality. The notion of the 'affair' is an aspect of the transformation undergone by sexuality after the Second World War. As Illouz (1998) shows, during this time the idea of sex for its own sake was legitimized and reinforced by political and social discourses, including feminism and gay liberation, a process which was supported by cultural discourses coming from the sphere of consumption.

Drawing on the literary tradition which reinforced the romantic narrative of '*le grand amour*', Illouz (1998: 176) cites the case of Flaubert's *Madame Bovary*. Illouz shows that Emma Bovary clearly believed that her relationship with Rodolphe was no mere 'affair' but instead was a prelude to the 'grand narrative' of *le grand amour*. Illouz insightfully comments on the fact that Emma was at the watershed between the 'modern Romantic sensibility' where lives were dominated by the 'life-long master narrative of love' and the postmodern era which was characterized by a series of self-contained affairs.

By contrast, the affair is viewed as a different form of intensity which Illouz (1998: 177) positions squarely within the postmodern condition. She argues that the affair can be seen as a postmodern expression of intensities or experiences, including pure sensations, desire and pleasure, which do not include reason. By contrast with the premodern era, romantic intensities have eliminated the issue of 'waiting' which characterized women's lives in the Victorian era, and removed the concept of the 'tragic' in relationships.

Illouz describes 'the affair' as postmodern in a number of respects, particularly their institutionalization of 'liminality'. Liminality can be described as being a transitionary concept which describes being between two stages, or transitioning to a new stage. It can be seen as the threshold separating one space from another. By 'liminality', Illouz shows in defining affairs that all of the affairs took place in geographic, institutional or temporal locations away from locations such as home and work and outside of family, marriage and job contexts. As Illouz (1998: 177) shows: 'This form of liminality provides postmodernity a defining rhetorical figure – the inversion of normative hierarchies and symbolic form – the *reversal* of identities and blurring of boundaries, social, aesthetic and cultural.'

In 'Love and its discontents: irony, reason, romance,' Illouz (2010: 21) develops the contrast between 'love at first sight' and 'postmodern love' further when she argues that the model of 'love at first sight' provides an example of what can be called an 'enchanted' version of love, that is, a view of love which goes beyond reason, to an intensely meaningful experience which exposes the self to an almost 'quasi-religious sense of transcendence' (Illouz, 2010: 21).

Such a model of 'enchanted love', Illouz notes, can be compared with a postmodern conception of love which is captured by Candace Bushnell's (1996: 2) *Sex and the City*:

> When was the last time you heard someone say 'I love you!' without tagging on the inevitable (if unspoken) 'as a friend'. When was the last time you saw two people gazing into each other's eyes without thinking, Yeah right! When was the last time you heard someone announce 'I am truly, madly in love', without thinking, just wait until Monday morning! (cited in Illouz, 2010: 22)

Illouz maintains that Bushnell's view presents a 'disenchanted' approach to love. She shows how this marks a shift from 'enchanted' to 'disenchanted' definitions of love. Illouz argues that Candace Bushnell presents a supremely ironic, self-conscious and 'disenchanted' approach to love. Illouz correctly identifies that Bushnell's (1996) *Sex and the City* is part of the growth of the 'chick-lit' genre which addressed the issues women experienced in relationships and, as such, it is a site where 'modern love has become the privileged site for the trope of irony (Illouz, 2010: 22). Illouz argues that the process of the rationalization or 'disenchantment' of love is central to this new ironic structure of romantic feeling which she maintains signals the move from an 'enchanted' to 'disenchanted' cultural definition of love.

This process of disenchantment or rationalization of love is linked with the emergence of the psy-sciences, which is part of a process which Illouz describes as 'making love into a science'. She maintains that this process undermines the cultural status of love.

Illouz claims that in the 20th and 21st centuries, the psy-sciences, including psychology, psychoanalysis, biology and evolutionary psychology, have attempted to explain love by such categories as 'the unconscious', 'hormones', 'survival of species' or 'brain chemistry'. Illouz argues that while psychoanalysis sees love as part of the fundamental constitution of the self, at the same time they undermine its cultural status by seeing it as derivative of psychic processes including 'psychic trauma', 'Oedipal conflict' or 'repetition compulsion'.

Perhaps one of the most famous quotations drawn from Illouz's (2010) article focuses on reducing love to brain chemistry as follows:

> Studies in neuroscience have suggested that a consistent number of chemicals are present in the brain when people testify to feeling love. These chemicals include; Testosterone, Estrogen, Dopamine, Norepinephrine, Serotonin, Oxytocin, and Vasopressin. For example, a dramatic increase in the amount of Dopamine and Norepinephrine is said to be present in the brain when one is infatuated with another person. More specifically, higher levels of Testosterone and Estrogen are present during the lustful phase of a relationship. Dopamine, Norepinephrine, and Serotonin are more commonly found during the attraction phase of a relationship ... Serotonin levels are also significantly higher in the brains of people who have recently fallen in love, than in the brains of others. Oxytocin and Vasopressin seem to be more closely linked to long-term bonding and relationships characterized by strong attachments. (Illouz, 2010: 25)

This is a fascinating summary of the interaction between different drugs and relationship states. As Illouz shows, love has been subjected to the same processes of 'disenchantment' as nature, and the scientific explanations reduce 'love to an epiphenomenon' (Illouz, 2010: 26).

A further dimension which has contributed to the rationalization process has been the overlap of internet technology with psychological knowledge and the impact of the market on choice. Illouz (2010) argues that the 'premodern actor' who was seeking a partner was rational, she considered factors such as dowry size, a possible partner's personal and family wealth and status, their education and political affiliation.

By comparison, Illouz (2010) shows that in postmodern society, a combination of internet technology, psychology and capitalism have produced a wider range of criteria which are applied to partner selection. She argues that the intersection of psychology, internet technology and the logic of the capitalist market has produced a much more self-conscious personality, who adopts a more refined set of criteria in order to establish a greater level of compatibility.

Of course, the most obvious area is that of online dating, and Illouz (2010) maintains that actors use elaborate rational strategies to achieve their romantic objectives. This tends to confirm Alexander's (2012) assertion that the impact of computer technology is to produce a rationalizing effect. The implications of this produces a situation where partners become interchangeable and can be improved upon whether in terms of age, income or status.

Illouz (2010: 29–30) recognizes that feminism has been central in influencing the cultural history of love. She argues that more than any political or cultural formation, feminism has been important in influencing the cultural history of love because it debunked the notion of male chivalry as well as the feminine mystique. In its challenge to structures of power, feminism also worked to establish ideals of equality, reciprocity and fairness.

Finally, Illouz (2012) shows that the feminist movement as a cultural movement developed rules of conduct that rationalized love and sexual relations in two important ways. Firstly, it called on women to become more aware of relationships of power within intimate bonds, and secondly, led to new ways of thinking more reflexively about romance.

Elsewhere, Illouz (2012) returns to some of the same issues raised earlier, but she becomes more explicitly critical of the psy-sciences as she comments: 'Clinical psychology has played a uniquely central role in suggesting (and bestowing scientific legitimacy on) the idea of love and its failures must be explained by the psychic history of the individual …' (Illouz, 2012: 4). She shows that feelings of hurt, demoralization and the devaluing of self were powerful in encouraging a host of professions, including psychoanalysts, psychologists and therapists as well as the media industries. She shows that feminists have sharply contested these views of psychic disorders and argues that it is not some bizarre explanation of dysfunctional childhood or underdeveloped psyches which are at fault, but instead, a set of social and cultural tensions that have come to define modern identities.

Illouz (2012) has correctly identified feminist writers and thinkers who have contested both the belief in love as the source of all happiness as well as the psychological individualist understanding of the often distressing nature of love.

Essentially, as Illouz shows, the issue is not about individual psyches but about power. Feminists argue that it is power which lies at the core of love and sexuality and that men have had, and continue to have, dominance in the struggle for power in relationships, because there is convergence between economic and sexual power. Illouz (2012: 9) sees love as central to the study of modernity and aligns her thinking with that of Giddens, Beck and Beck-Gernsheim and Bauman.

Illouz maintains that heterosexual romantic love embodies two of the cultural revolutions of the 20th century, the first is the individualization of lifestyles and the intensification of emotional life, as outlined by these social theorists. Secondly, the 'economization of social relationships' in the way that the self is shaped by economic factors.

She makes the important point that there is a direct relationship between heterosexual love and social mobility. Illouz (2012) maintains that there is an intersection of the economic and the emotional, as well as the romantic and the rational, in the emergence of the modern individual. She argues that this is the case because the importance of love in marriage (and she argues, in the novel) coincided with the decline of marriage as a vehicle for family alliances and highlighted a new significance of love within social mobility.

She draws on Giddens and others to show that love played a central role in female autonomy.

Love was important for women, because following patterns established by men, it did so by reinforcing a model of the self that was individualistic, private and domestic and established 'emotional autonomy'. As Illouz (2012: 12) notes, 'in fact, love is the paradigmatic example and the very engine of a new model of sociability dubbed by Giddens as that of the "pure relationship"'. She also makes an important point as regards sociology's need to remain relevant, in saying that sociology should include an analysis of the emotions in order to show 'the vulnerability of the self' in late modernity. She argues that this vulnerability is both emotional and institutional.

True to the title of her monograph, *Why Love Hurts: A Sociological Explanation*, Illouz (2012: 16) argues that there is something new in the kind of experience emanating from the pain generated by love. She argues that what is different or properly modern in the idea of suffering, emerging from romance, is what she calls 'the deregulation of marriage markets'. In other words, there are changes to the scope of choice in the selection of partners and the criteria people adopt in their choices (see also Brooks, 2017, 2019a). Love becomes significant in the overall importance of a social sense of worth, in the rationalization of passion, and in the ways in which romance is understood and responded to.

Illouz describes changes in ritual patterns surrounding romantic encounters, and describes the ritual of 'calling' in early to mid-19th-century England. The ritual of 'calling' is described by Illouz (2012) as follows:

> 'Calling' was such a ritual. It took place at the girl's home … which therefore made it inappropriate for a man to take the initiative in calling. A man could show a girl that he liked her, but it was the girl's 'privilege' to ask a man to call. The middle-class practice of calling on a woman gave the parents and the woman herself control over the courtship process. (Illouz, 2012: 29)

In addition, 'similarly, if a gentleman was introduced to a lady at a party for the purpose of dancing, he could not automatically resume the acquaintance on the street. He had to be reintroduced by a mutual friend and be permitted by the woman to resume contact' (Illouz, 2012: 29).

The key issue here and around the middle-class practice of 'calling' was it gave control to the parents and woman in managing the romantic encounter. Illouz (2012: 30) characterizes this organization of the emotions as a 'regime of performativity of emotions', 'that is, a regime in which emotions are induced by the ritualized actions and expressions of sentiments'. Interestingly, Illouz (2012: 31) contrasts this 'regime of performativity of emotions' with what she describes as 'a regime of emotional authenticity' which she states pervades modern relationships; she describes this in the following way: 'authenticity demands that actor know their feelings; that they act on such feelings …; that people reveal their feelings to themselves; and that they make decisions about relationships and commit themselves based on these feelings.'

Illouz describes this as 'the great transformation of love' and characterizes these changes within an 'architecture of romantic choice'. This latter concept includes a number of factors. Firstly, the deregulation of normative patterns in the way in which prospective partners are assessed. Secondly, the tendency to understand one's sexual or romantic partner at the same time in psychological terms. In other words, to have full exposure to a potential partner's psychological make-up and sexual proclivities. Finally, the emergence of what Illouz calls 'sexual fields', where sexuality is seen to play an important role in how individuals compete in the marriage market.

Thus, the shift in the choice of 'a mate' encapsulates a broader range of criteria including 'emotional intimacy', 'psychological compatibility' and 'sexiness'. It is this latter dimension which has possibly been the most transformative, as Illouz (2012: 42) shows. The dimension of sexiness has become an autonomous and important factor in the selection of a mate. Illouz (2012) argues that this has emerged as a result of consumerism and the increasing normative importance of sexuality as defined by both psychological and by feminist cultural perspectives. In summary, Illouz (2012: 53) shows that 'erotic attractiveness and sexual performance mark the rise of new ways of bestowing social value in marriage markets. Sexuality thus becomes closely intertwined with social value.'

## Part III. 'Mediated intimacy' in heterosexual men

One of the key issues characterizing most theoretical work and empirical research undertaken by feminists and others is the focus on women in heterosexual relationships. One exception to the rule is Rachel O'Neill's (2015b) interesting work on heterosexual men involved in the London 'seduction community'. As she (2015b: 1) outlines: 'herein, heterosexual men undertake various forms of skills training and personal development in order to gain greater choice and control in their relationships with women …'. She examines 'how men who participate in this setting engage a mode of intimate subjectivity ordered by themes of management and enterprise.'

In doing so, O'Neill sets out to understand the 'seduction community' as what she calls a site of 'mediated intimacy' which she argues must be set in the context of wider cultural rationalities which have been generated by neoliberal capitalism. The 'seduction community' has been imported from the US and O'Neill claims it has occupied a presence in London for the last 17 years.

O'Neill assesses seduction as 'mediated intimacy' and states that it was identified by Ken Plummer almost 20 years ago. Her interest focuses on the representations of intimate relations and how these proliferate across the mass media. This isn't in itself 'ground breaking' research, but O'Neill's focus on the 'seduction community' is novel. This is reflected in a broader strategy related to what she calls 'a kind of grammar of mediation', 'such that all mediated life becomes refracted through a lens of intimacy in a way that is distinct from earlier moments' (Tyler and Gill, 2013: 80). O'Neill is interested in the mediation of contemporary intimate life and the ways in which intimate and sexual subjectivities are defined by social and cultural rationalities, in particular, postfeminism and neoliberalism.

Drawing on Gill's (2009) work, O'Neill (2015b) shows how this operates for women. Gill maintains that sexual subjectivity and intimate relations become the focus of sites of labour and investment. Gill focuses specifically on the advice given on sex and relationships by women's magazines. In the process, Gill identifies both 'representational patterns' and 'discursive repertoires', including 'intimate entrepreneurships' which she (Gill) argues occur when sex and relationships are planned for, organized and managed meticulously.

She also identifies 'men-ology', where women are given instructions in how to appeal to and please men, and finally 'transforming the self', where women are encouraged to rethink how they understand their bodies and their desires. In addition, she also identifies the kinds of sexual practices they engage in, as well as the intimate relationships they have with men. Gill shows how this range of discourses and practices highlight the operation of what she calls 'neoliberal rationalities' as they apply to intimate life, in that women are repeatedly encouraged to work on and develop their 'sexual selves' and to build up an 'intimate skill set' (O'Neill, 2015b: 7).

O'Neill (2015b) also shows that while it is the case that both women and men are encouraged to become 'enterprising sexual subjects', the discourses are gendered with what O'Neill describes as 'masculine repertoires', defined in terms of scientific rationality and efficiency as defined by Harvey and Gill (2011), as well as in terms of planning and strategy as defined by

Farvid and Braun (2013). O'Neill (2015b: 9) makes the point that there has been too little scholarship on the intersection of neoliberal rationalities and men's sexual practices and how men understand a social and cultural context, where feminism is understood and at the same time is taken apart.

Drawing on the work of Illouz (2014), O'Neill describes seduction training as practised by the 'seduction community' as 'yet another form of "serial recreational sexuality organized under the aegis of the market" (Illouz, 2014: 4)' (O'Neill, 2015b: 14).

Illouz (2014) highlights the fact that romance provides a competitive romantic field where practices are highly competitive. For example, O'Neill argues that the idea of the 'pick-up' is seen as a means for some men to take advantage of others. She maintains that this was a common sentiment expressed by several of the men she interviewed. Drawing on one of the people interviewed, he described how he feels after completing a 'pick-up training' course. A university student called Antonio explains that after 'the bootcamp' he feels he has moved from being disadvantaged to totally advantaged. As O'Neill notes, in these cases nothing could be further removed from the concept of 'democratic bargaining' of the 'pure relationship' envisioned by Beck and Beck-Gernsheim ([1995] 2002) and Giddens (1992); here, heterosexual relationships are framed by a more competitive ethos characterized by individualism.

In O'Neill's (2015b: 17) research, she found that the responses of these heterosexual men were consistent in their expectations of women. O'Neill observes there was an overall uniformity in the way men responded. In addition, these men described a 'feminine ideal' in stereotypical terms which reflects contemporary media advertising, as follows: 'young, slim, and able-bodies, normatively white or an exoticised "other" and conventionally attractive'. Additionally, there was an emphasis on women being 'fit', with men following the usual stereotypical model of preferring women who exercise regularly and visit the gym, as well as taking care of themselves more generally.

O'Neill shows in her research how 'forms of intimate and sexual subjectivity negotiated by men who participate in this community – industry-ordered by logics of enterprise and management, competition and consumerism – have resonance with broader patterns of subjectivity and sociality elaborated in neoliberal capitalism' (O'Neill, 2015b: 18). It also contests the narrative which presents men involved in the 'seduction community' as 'pathetic, pathological or perverse – an army of sleazebags, saddos and weirdos (Freeman, 2014)'. O'Neill raises concerns that there is a reconfiguration of intimate and sexual subjectivities, producing 'antisocial forms of sociability' which are directly related to neoliberal rationalities. She argues that this may be conducive to sexual coercion and violence, 'particularly in a context where gender equality is assumed to have been achieved and women are imbued with "compulsory sexual agency" (Burkett and Hamilton, 2012; Gill 2008b, 2008a)' (O'Neill, 2015b: 18).

Almost all of the empirical research in the area of intimacy has tended to focus on the West. However, there is some interesting empirical research which draws on other cultural contexts, particularly Southeast Asia.

An article by Strijbosch (2015) on the influence of Singapore, as a city state, on intimate heterosexual relationships, particularly on young, single, well-educated women, provides some interesting elements. Strijbosch indicates that Singapore faces low birth rates, late marriage and high rates of non-marriage within society more generally. As Strijbosch (2015: 1108) shows: 'the number of people staying "effectively single" in their 30s is even higher than late-marrying countries in Europe (Jones, 2012a)'.

The study focuses on how young, well-educated, single women experience intimacy in Singapore and how they negotiate and experience family ideals against attitudes towards intimacy and relationships. Strijbosch (2015: 1109) argues that 'well-educated women are relevant to investigate because they are together with less educated men statistically the group most likely to remain single (Jones, 2012a: 93)'.

The statistics show that in 2010, 62 per cent of women between the ages of 25 and 29 who held a university degree were single. For men with a similar educational background and age, 76 per cent were also single in 2010. Drawing on Jones (2012a), Strijbosch (2015) shows that in the age category 30–34 years old, 28 per cent of women and 35 per cent of men with a university degree were single. Women between the ages of 30 and 34 who had less than a secondary degree were single in up to 13 per cent of cases. In 2010, for men in the same age group with less than secondary education, 40 per cent were single (see Strijbosch, 2015: 1109). The state is highly interventionist in Singapore as is well documented (Wong and Yeoh, 2003) and is particularly concerned about the low fertility rates among the Chinese Singaporean population.

Strijbosch (2015) is correct to note that:

> Individuals in Singapore usually decide who their marriage partner is, and people often meet through their own social networks. This, however does not mean that familial notions are unimportant. As Chan and Xu (2007: 101) outline, family control and obligations are part of the process of getting married as well. (Strijbosch, 2015: 1110)

There are a large number of international marriages in Singapore and Strijbosch notes that: 'The countries with the highest proportion of international marriages in East and Southeast Asia are Taiwan, Singapore and South Korea (Jones and Shen, 2008: 13). In Singapore, 40% of all marriages involve a non-Singaporean person (Jones, 2012a: 3)' (Strijbosch, 2015: 1110).

In addition, Strijbosch also shows that 97 per cent of males who marry internationally, will marry Asian women, whereas only 69 per cent of female citizens who marry internationally do so. Jones (2012a) shows that 25 per cent of these bridegrooms come from America, Europe and Oceania. The dominant profile as indicated by Strijbosch (2015) is that male Singaporeans are marrying foreigners (see Yeoh, Leng and Dung, 2013: 145).

It is argued that the reason for these differences can be explained by the different profiles of male and female Singaporean citizens marrying non-Singaporeans. Strijbosch (2015) argues for males, 52.5 per cent have a post-secondary education or university education. Almost 75 per cent of females marrying non-Singaporeans, while they have these levels of education, are marrying men with even higher levels of education (see Jones, 2012a).

One of the ways in which the Singaporean state tries to control marriages is through their control of government-subsidized housing. Singles in Singapore cannot individually live in government-subsidized flats until they are 35 years old. The government-subsidized housing is called HDB flats. The age limitation for access to HDB flats 'incentivizes young couples to marry and settle down, given that the possibility of affording a private house is limited by the scarcity of land and the high prices of private houses (Ong, 2000: 50)' (Strijbosch, 2015: 1113).

Singapore is also a highly consumerist society. 'In cultures, where capitalism and emotions are highly intertwined, emotions have become entities to be evaluated, discussed, bargained, and commodified (Illouz, 2007: 108–9)' (Strijbosch, 2015: 1121). It is claimed that it is the shrinking pool of women who meet the expectations of Singaporean men, and vice versa, which explains why many Singaporeans are looking for foreign spouses.

There are a number of myths surrounding why Asian women only date White men. One of the women interviewed in Strijbosch's (2015) research, Valeria, had the following comments:

'It is an Asian girl who only dates White men. She does not even bother to date local men, she dates White men usually because she perceives them to be rich.' According to Valeria, it is a myth that girls are interested only in money and the status of *Ang moh* (Caucasian men). Singaporean women are also interested in these men because they think Caucasian men have more egalitarian gender ideals: 'A Singaporean guy's mindset can be quite traditional. They want to be the leader. We woman want to be equal. Western guys do not expect girls to serve them and tend to be more open minded'. (Strijbosch, 2015: 1122)

Strijbosch (2015) accurately notes the pressures and contradictions within which women are placed:

> On the one hand, women are expected to study, have a career, and develop themselves as autonomous, critical people, whereas on the other hand, it is expected that in a relationship one should not be too expressive, earn less than a partner, and not drink, smoke or party too much. (Strijbosch, 2015: 1122)

Thus there are inherent contradictions within the lives of well-educated Singaporean women who are balancing familial expectations alongside their desire to establish successful relationships.

## In summary

Chapter 7 has reviewed a broad range of theories and theorists from feminism, cultural theory and sociology who have engaged with the relationship of emotions, love and intimacy. The chapter adopted a socio-historical perspective in considering the debates and contributions to the field from a consideration of romantic love and the emergence of intimacy, through a consideration of love as a postmodern condition to the analysis of 'mediated intimacy' in heterosexual men. The chapter has provided a comprehensive and wide-ranging analysis of this rich and fascinating field.

# Bibliography

Abu-Lughod, L. (1986) *Veiled Sentiments: Honor and Poetry in a Bedouin Society*, Berkeley: University of California Press.

Adorno, T. (2005) [1951] *Minima Moralia: Reflections from a Damaged Life*, London: Verso.

Ahall, L. (2018) 'Affect as methodology: feminism and the politics of emotion', *International Political Sociology*, 12(1): 36–52.

Ahall, L. and Gregory, T. (2013) 'Security, emotions, affect', *Critical Studies on Security,* 1(1): 117–20.

Ahall, L. and Gregory, T. (eds) (2015) *Emotions, Politics and War,* London/New York: Routledge.

Ahmed, S. (2004) *The Cultural Politics of Emotions*, New York: Routledge.

Ahmed, S. (2007) 'Multiculturalism and the promise of happiness', *New Formations*, 63(1): 121–37.

Ahmed, S. (2008) 'The happiness turn', *New Formations*, 63(1): 7–14.

Ahmed, S. (2010) *The Promise of Happiness*, Durham, NC: Duke University Press.

Ahmed, S. (2014) 'Afterword: emotions and their objects', in *The Cultural Politics of Emotions*, Edinburgh: Edinburgh University Press, pp 204–33.

Albrecht, G., Sartore, G-M. and Pollard, G. (2007) 'Solastalgia: The Distress Caused by Environmental Change', *Australian Psychiatry*, 15(1): S95–98.

Alexander, J. (2012) *Trauma: A Social Theory*, Cambridge: Polity Press.

Alice, L. (1995) 'Feminism, Postmodernism, Postfeminism: A Space for an Encounter Between Feminist and Postfeminist Thinking', *Women's Studies Programme*, Massey University, New Zealand.

Althusser, L. (1971) 'Ideology and the ideological state apparatuses', in L. Althusser (ed) *Lenin and Philosophy and Other Essays*, London: New Left Books, pp 142–47.

Amichai-Hamburger, Y. and Ben-Artzi, E. (2003) 'Loneliness and internet use', *Computers in Human Behaviour*, 19(1): 71–80.

Anderson, E. (2009) *Inclusive Masculinity: The Changing Nature of Masculinities*, London/NY: Routledge.

Anderson, E. (2011) 'Masculinities and Sexualities in Sport and Physical Culture: Three Decades of Evolving Research', *Journal of Homosexuality*, 58: 565–78.

Archer, M.S. (2003) *Structure, Agency and the Internal Conversation*, Cambridge: Cambridge University Press.
Archer, M.S. (2007) *Making Our Way Through the World: Human Reflexivity and Social Mobility*, Cambridge: Cambridge University Press.
Archer, M.S. (2012) *The Promise of Happiness*, Durham, NC: Duke University Press.
Banet-Weiser, S. (2015) 'Whom are we empowering? Popular feminism and the work of empowerment' [conference paper], Console-ing Passions Conference, Dublin, 18 June 2015 (unpublished).
Banet-Weiser, S. (2018) *Empowered: Popular Feminism and Popular Misogyny*, Durham, NC: Duke University Press.
Barbalet, J. (1999) 'Boredom and social meaning', *British Journal of Sociology*, 50(4): 631–46.
Barbalet, J. (ed) (2002) *Emotions and Sociology*, Oxford: Blackwell.
Barbalet, J. (2004) *Emotion, Social Theory, and Social Structure: A Macrosociological Approach*, Cambridge: Cambridge University Press.
Barbalet, J. (2009) 'A characterization of trust and its consequences', *Theory and Society*, 38(4): 367–82.
Baudrillard, J. (2005) *The Intelligence of Evil or the Lucidity Pact*, New York: Palgrave.
Bauman, Z. (1991) *Modernity and Ambivalence*, Cambridge: Polity Press.
Bauman, Z. (1996) 'From pilgrim to tourist – or a short history of identity', in S. Hall and P.D. Gay (eds) *Questions of Cultural Identity*, London: Sage, pp 18–36.
Bauman, Z. (2000) *Liquid Modernity*, Cambridge: Polity Press.
Bauman, Z. (2003) *Liquid Love: On the Frailty of Human Bonds*, Cambridge: Polity.
Bauman, Z. (2004) *Wasted Lives: Modernity and its Outcasts*, Cambridge: Polity Press.
Bauman, Z. (2005) *Liquid Life*, Cambridge: Polity Press.
Bauman, Z. (2007) *Consuming Life*, Cambridge: Polity.
Beck, U. (1992) *Risk Society*, London: Sage.
Beck, U. (1994) *Ecological Enlightenment: Essays on the Politics of the Risk Society*, Amherst, NY: Prometheus Books.
Beck, U. and Beck-Gernsheim, E. (2002) [1995] *The Normal Chaos of Love*, Cambridge: Polity Press.
Beck, U., Giddens, A. and Lash, S. (1994) *Reflexive Modernization: Politics, Tradition and Aesthetics in the Modern Social Order*, Cambridge: Polity Press.
Bentham, J. (1969) [1789] 'An introduction to the principles of morals and legislation', in M. Warnock (ed) *Utilitarianism*, Glasgow: The Fontana Library.
Bericat, E. (2000) 'La sociologia y la emacion en la sociologia', *Papers: Revista de Sociologia*, 62: 145–76.

Bericat, E. (2005) 'La cultura del horror en la sociedades avanzadas: de la socieded centripeta a la Sociedad centrifuga', *Revista Espanola de Investigaciones Sociologicas*, 110(1): 53–89.

Bericat, E. (2016) 'The sociology of emotions: four decades of progress', *Current Sociology*, 64(3): 491–513.

Berlant, L. (1993) 'The queen of America goes to Washington City: Harriet Jacobs, Frances Harper, Anita Hill', *American Literature*, 65(3): 549–74.

Berlant, L. (ed) (2000) *Intimacy*, Chicago: University of Chicago Press.

Berlant, L. (2004) 'Two girls, fat and thin,' in S.M. Barber and D.I. Clarke (eds) *Regarding Sedgwick: Essays on Queer Culture and Critical Theory*, New York: Routledge.

Berlant, L. (2007a) 'Cruel optimism: on Marx, loss and the senses', *New Formations*, 63(1).

Berlant, L. (2007b) 'Nearly utopian, nearly normal: post-Fordist affect in *La Promesse* and *Rosetta*', *Public Culture*, 19(2): 273–301.

Berlant, L. (2009) *The Female Complaint: The Unfinished Business of Sentimentality in American Culture*, Durham, NC: Duke University Press.

Berlant, L. (2011) *Cruel Optimism*, Durham, NC: Duke University Press.

Bernstein, E. (2007) *Temporarily Yours: Intimacy, Authenticity and the Commerce of Sex,* Chicago: University of Chicago Press.

Bloch, M. (1992) *The Historian's Craft*, Manchester: Manchester University Press.

Boden, S. and Williams, S.J. (2002) 'Consumption and Emotion: The Romantic Ethic Revisited', *Sociology*, 36(3). https://doi.org/10.1177/0038038502036003001

Bok, D. (2010) *The Politics of Happiness. What Government Can Learn from the New Research on Well-being*, Princeton and Oxford: Princeton University Press.

Boltanski, L. and Chiapello, E. (2007) [1997] *The New Spirit of Capitalism*, London: Verso.

Bordo, S. (1993) *Unbearable Weight: Feminism, Western Culture, and the Body*, Berkeley: University of California Press.

Bourdieu, P. (1984) *Distinction: A Social Critique of the Judgement of Taste*, London: Routledge and Kegan Paul.

Bourdieu, P. (1998) *Practical Reason*, Cambridge: Polity Press.

Bourdieu, P. (2001) *Masculine Domination*, Cambridge: Polity Press.

Braidotti, R. (1991) *Patterns of Dissonance: A Study of Women in Contemporary Philosophy*, Cambridge: Polity Press.

Braidotti, R. (2006) *Transpositions: On Nomadic Ethics*, Cambridge: Polity Press.

Brannen, J. and Moss, P. (1991) *Managing Mothers: Dual Earner Households After Maternity Leave*, London: Allen and Unwin.

Brennan, T. (2004) *The Transmission of Affect*, New York: Cornell University Press.

Brooks, A. (1997) *Postfeminisms: Feminism, Cultural Theory and Cultural Forms*, London/New York: Routledge.

Brooks, A. (2008) 'Reconceptualising reflexivity and dissonance in professional and personal domains', *British Journal of Sociology*, 59(3): 539–59.

Brooks, A. (2010) *Social Theory in Contemporary Asia: Intimacy, Reflexivity and Identity*, London: Routledge.

Brooks, A. (2014) '"The affective turn" in the social sciences and the gendered nature of emotions: theorizing emotions in the social sciences from 1800 to the present', in D. Lemmings and A. Brooks (eds) *Emotions and Social Change: Historical and Sociological Perspectives*, New York: Routledge.

Brooks, A. (2017) *Genealogies of Emotions, Intimacies and Desire: Theories of Changes in Emotional Regimes from Medieval Society to Late Modernity*, London/New York: Routledge.

Brooks, A. (2019a) *Love and Intimacy in Contemporary Society: International Perspectives on Love*, London/New York: Routledge.

Brooks, A. (2019b) *Women, Politics and the Public Sphere*, London: Bristol University Press/Policy Press.

Brooks, A. (2022) '*Big Little Lies* – feminist or postfeminist fiction? The subversion of the love discourse in Liane Moriarty's novel and in the series', in A. Brooks (ed) *The Routledge Companion to Romantic Love*, London/New York: Routledge, pp 96–114.

Brooks, A. and Wee, L. (2008) 'Reflexivity and the transformation of gender identity: reviewing the potential for change in a cosmopolitan society', *Sociology*, 42(3): 503–21.

Brooks, A. and Simpson, R. (2012) *Emotions in Transmigration: Transformation, Movement and Identity*, London: Palgrave Macmillan.

Bruckner, P. (2000) [1997] *Perpetual Euphoria: On the Day to be Happy*, Princeton, NJ: Princeton University Press.

Burkett, M. and Hamilton, K. (2012) 'Postfeminist Sexual Agency: Young Women's Negotiations of Sexual Consent', *Sexualities*, 15(7): 815–833.

Burkitt, I. (1997) 'Social relationships and emotions', *Sociology*, 31(1): 37–55.

Burkitt, I. (2002) 'Complex emotions: relations, feelings and images in emotional experience', in J. Barbalet (ed) *Emotions and Sociology*, Oxford: Blackwell, pp 151–68.

Burkitt, I. (2012) 'Emotional reflexivity: feeling, emotion and imagination in reflexive dialogues', *Sociology*, 46(3): 458–72.

Bushnell, C. (1996) *Sex and the City*, New York: Atlantic Monthly Press.

Butler, J. (1990) *Gender Trouble: Feminism and the Subversion of Identity*, London: Routledge.

Butler, J. (1997) *Excitable Speech: A Politics of the Performative*, New York: Routledge.

Butler, J. (2004) *Precarious Life: The Power of Mourning and Violence*, London: Verso.

Butler, J. (2011) *Bodies that Matter. On the Discursive Limits of Sex*, London: Routledge.

Butler, J. (2013) 'For white girls only: Postfeminism and the politics of inclusion', *Feminist Formations*, 25(1): 35–8.

Cabanas, E. and Illouz, E. (2016) 'The making of a "happy worker": positive psychology in neoliberal organizations', in A.J. Pugh (ed) *Beyond the Cubicle: Insecurity Culture and the Flexible Self*, New York: Oxford University Press.

Cabanas, E. and Illouz, E. (2019) 'Hijacking the language of functionality?: in praise of "negative" emotions against happiness', in N. Hill et al (eds) *Critical Happiness Studies,* London: Routledge.

Calhoun, C. (2001) 'Putting emotions in their place', in J. Goodwin, J.M. Jasper and F. Polletta (eds) *Passionate Politics: Emotions and Social Movements*, Chicago: University of Chicago Press, pp 45–57.

Cancian, F. (1987) *Love in America: Gender and Self -Development*, Cambridge: Cambridge University Press.

Carroll, J. (2001) *The Western Dreaming,* Sydney: Harper Collins.

Chan, S.C. and Xu, S.M. (2007) 'Wedding photographs and the bridal gaze in Singapore', *New Zealand Journal of Asian Studies*, 9: 87–103.

Charmaz, K. and Milligan, M.J. (2006) 'Grief', in J.E. Stets and J.H. Turner (eds) *Handbook of the Sociology of Emotions*, Boston, MA: Springer, pp 679–711.

Clark, C. (1987) 'Sympathy biography and sympathy margin', *American Journal of Sociology*, 93(2): 263–89.

Clearly, A. (2012) 'Suicidal action, emotional expression, and the performance of masculinities', *Social Science and Medicine*, 74: 498–505.

Colebrook, C. (2007) 'Narrative happiness and the meaning of life', *New Formations,* 63(1).

Collett, J.L. and Lizardo, O. (2010) 'Occupational status and the experiences of anger', *Social Forces*, 88(5): 2079–104.

Connell, R.W. (1995) *Masculinities*, Cambridge: Polity Press.

Cottingham, M.D. (2015) 'Learning to "deal" and "de-escalate": how men in nursing manage self and patient emotions', *Sociological Inquiry*, 85(1): 75–99.

Cottingham, M. (2016) 'Theorizing emotional capital', *Theory and Society*, 45(5): 451–70.

Cvetkovich, A. (1992) *Mixed Feelings: Feminism, Mass Culture, and Victorian Sensationalism*, New Jersey: Rutgers University Press.

Cvetkovich, A. (2003) *An Archive of Feelings: Trauma, Sexuality and Lesbian Public Cultures*, North Carolina: Duke University Press.

Cvetkovich, A. (2012) 'Depression is ordinary: Public feelings and Saidiya Hartman's *Lose Your Mother*', *Feminist Theory*, 13(2): 131–46.

Davies, W. (2015) *The Happiness Industry: How the Government and Big Business Sold U.S. Well-Being*, London: Verso.

Davis, M. (2008) 'Bauman on globalization – the human consequences of a liquid world' in M.H. Jacobsen and P. Poder (eds) *The Sociology of Zygmunt Bauman: Challenges and Critiques,* Hampshire: Ashgate, pp 1–29.

Dean, M. (1994) *Governmentality*. Oxford: Oxford University Press.

De Boise, S. and Hearn, J. (2017) 'Are men getting more emotional?: Critical sociological perspectives on men, masculinities and emotions', *The Sociological Review*, 65(4): 779–96.

De Lauretis, T. (1987) *Technologies of Gender: Essays on Theory, Film and Fiction*, Indiana: Indiana University Press.

Deleuze, G. (1997) 'Immanence: A Life…' *Theory, Culture and Society*, 14(2): 3–7.

Denzin, N.K. (2007) *On Understanding Emotion*, New Jersey: Transaction Publishers.

Douglas, M. (2002) *Purity and Danger*, London: Routledge.

De Riviera, J. (1992) 'Emotional climate: social structure and emotional dynamics', in K.T. Strongman (ed) *International Review of Studies on Emotion*, ii, pp 197–218.

Duby, G. (1994) *Love and Marriage in the Middle Ages*, Chicago: University of Chicago Press.

Duncan, G. (2019) 'Happiness and the new politics of subjectivity', in N. Hill, S. Brinkmann and A. Peterson (eds) *Critical Happiness Studies*, London: Routledge, pp 83–97.

Durkheim, E. (1964) *The Division of Labour in Society*, New York: The Free Press.

Dutt, A.K. and Radcliff, B. (2009) (eds) *Happiness, Economics and Politics*, Radcliff: University of Notre Dame.

Durr, M. and Wingfield, A.H. (2011) 'Keep your "N" in check! African American women and the interactive effects of etiquette and emotional labour', *Critical Sociology*, 37(5): 557–71.

Elias, A. (2016) 'Beautiful Body, Confident Soul: Young Women and the Beauty Labour of Neoliberalism', unpublished PhD thesis, Kings College London.

Elias, A., Gill, R. and Scharff, C. (eds) (2017) *Aesthetic Labour: Beauty Politics in Neoliberalism*, London: Palgrave/Macmillan.

Elias, N. (1978/1982) *The Civilizing Process*, Oxford: Blackwell.

Farvid, P. and Braun, V. (2013) 'Casual sex as "not a natural act" and other regimes of truth about heterosexuality', *Feminism and Psychology*, 23(3): 359–78.

Farvid, P., Braun, V. and Rowney, C. (2017) '"No girl wants to be called a slut": Women, heterosexual casual sex and the sexual double standard', *Journal of Gender Studies*, 26(5): 544–60.

Flood, M. (2005) 'Mapping loneliness in Australia', discussion paper 76, The Australian Institute, Canberra.

Forgas, J. (2013) 'Don't worry, be sad! On the cognitive, motivational and interpersonal benefits of negative mood', *Current Directions in Psychological Science*, 22(3): 225–32.

Forrest, A. (2010) 'Citizenship, Honour and Masculinity: Military Qualities under the French Revolution and Empire', in K. Hagemann, G. Mettle and J. Rendall (eds) *Gender, War and Politics: War Culture and Society*, 1750–1850, London: Palgrave Macmillan, pp 93-109.

Foucault, M. (1965) *Madness and Civilization*, New York: Pantheon Books.

Foucault, M. (1977) *Discipline and Punish: The Birth of the Prison*, New York: Vintage Books.

Foucault, M. (1988) *Technologies of the Self: A Seminar with Michael Foucault*, London: Tavistock.

Franklin, A.S. and Tranter, B. (2011) 'Loneliness, housing and health', *Australian Housing and Urban Research*, Final Report 164, Melbourne: Australian Housing and Urban Research Institute.

Franklin, A.S., Barbosa Neves, B., Jaworski, K., Hookway, N., Patulny, R. and Tranter, B. (2019) 'Towards an understanding of loneliness among Australian men: gender culture, embodied expression and the social bases of belonging', *Journal of Sociology*, 55(1): 124–43.

Fraser, N. (2013) *Fortunes of Feminism: From State-managed Capitalism to Neoliberal Crisis*, London: Verso Books.

Freedman, P. (1998) 'Peasant anger in the Middle Ages', in B.H. Rosenwein (ed) *Anger's Past: The Social Uses of an Emotion in the Middle Ages*, New York: Cornell University Press.

Freeman, H. (2014) 'Women Beware this PUA Army of Sleazebags, Saddos and Weirdos', *The Guardian Online*, Wednesday 12 November.

Frey, B. and Stutzer, A. (2009) 'Happiness and Public Choice', *Public Choice*, 144(3): 557–73.

Friedan, B. (1984) *The Feminine Mystique*, New York: Dell Publishing.

Galasinski, D. (2004) *Men and the Language of Emotions*, Basingstoke: Palgrave.

Garcia-Favaro, L. (2016) 'Confidence chic', in A. Elias, R. Gill and C. Schaff (eds) *Aesthetic Labour: Rethinking Beauty Politics in Neoliberal and Postfeminist Times*, London: Palgrave, 283–300.

Giddens, A. (1990) *The Consequences of Modernity*, Palo Alto, CA.: Stanford University Press.

Giddens, A. (1991) *Modernity and Self-Identity: Self and Society in the Late Modern Age*, Cambridge: Polity.

Giddens, A. (1992) *The Transformation of Intimacy: Sexuality, Love and Eroticism in Modern Societies*, Palo Alto, CA.: Stanford University Press.

Gill, R. (2008a) 'Culture and Subjectivity in Neoliberal and Postfeminist Times', *Subjectivity*, 25: 432–45.

Gill, R. (2008b) 'Empowerment/Sexism: Figuring Female Sexual Agency in Contemporary Advertising', *Feminism and Psychology*, 18: 35–60.

Gill, R. (2009) 'Beyond the "sexualization of culture" thesis: An intersectional analysis of "sixpacks", "midriffs" and "hot lesbians" in advertising', *Sexualities*, 12(2): 137–60.

Gill, R. (2017) 'The affective, cultural and psychic life of postfeminism: a postfeminist sensibility 10 years on', *European Journal of Cultural Studies*, 20(6): 606–26.

Gill, R. and Donaghue, N. (2013) 'As if Postfeminism Had Come True: The Turn to Agency in Cultural Studies of "Sexualisation"', in A. Phillips, S. Madhok and K. Wilson (eds) *Gender, Agency and Coercion*. London: Palgrave.

Gill, R. and Kanai, A. (2018) 'Mediating neoliberal capitalism: affect, subjectivity and inequality', *Journal of Communication*, 68(2): 318–26.

Gill, R. and Orgad, S. (2015) 'The confidence cult(ure)', *Australian Feminist Studies*, 30(86): 324–44.

Gill, R. and Orgad, S. (2017) 'Confidence culture and the remaking of feminism', *New Formations,* 91: 16–34.

Gill, R. and Scharff, C. (eds) (2011) *New Femininities: Postfeminism, Neoliberalism and Subjectivity*, London: Palgrave/Macmillan.

Goodwin, J., Jasper, J.M. and Polletta, F. (2014) *Passionate Politics: Emotions and Social Movements,* Chicago: University of Chicago Press.

Gorton, K. (2007) 'Theorizing emotion and affect: feminist engagements', *Feminist Theory,* 8(3): 333–48.

Gramsci, A. (1971) *Selections from the Prison Notebooks*, London: Lawrence and Wishart.

Greco, M. and Stenner, P. (eds) (2008) *Emotions: A Social Science Reader*, London/New York: Routledge.

Gregory, T. (2012) 'Potential lives, impossible death', *International Feminist Journal of Politics*, 14(3): 327–47.

Gregory, T. and Ahall, L. (2015) 'Introduction: mapping emotions, politics and war', in L. Ahall and T. Gregory (eds) *Emotions, Politics and War*, London/New York: Routledge.

Gross, N. (2005) 'The detraditionalization of intimacy reconsidered', *Sociological Theory*, 23(3): 286–311.

Gwynne, J. and Muller, N. (2013) *Postfeminism and Contemporary Hollywood Cinema*, Basingstoke: Palgrave.

Habermas, J. (1985) *The Theory of Communicative Action, Volume two: Lifeworld and System: A Critique of Functionalist Reason*, Boston, MA: Beacon Press.

Habermas, J. (1990) *Moral Consciousness and Communicative Action*, Cambridge: Polity Press.

Hall, S. (1986) 'Variants of liberalism', in J. Donald and S. Hall (eds) *Politics and Ideology*, Buckingham: Open University Press.

Hardt, M. and Negri, A. (2006) *Multitude: War and Democracy in the Age of Empire*, London: Hamish Hamilton.

Harvey, D. (2005) *A Brief History of Neoliberalism*, Oxford: Oxford University Press.

Harvey, L. and Gill, R. (2011) 'Spicing it up: sexual entrepreneurs and sex inspectors', in R. Gill and C. Schaff (eds) *New Femininities: Postfeminism, Neoliberalism and Identity*, Basingstoke: Palgrave, pp 52–67.

Hazleden, R. (2004) 'The pathology of love in contemporary relationship manuals', *The Sociological Review*, 52(2): 201–17.

Heller, D. (ed) (2007) *Makeover Television: Reality Remodelled*, London: IB Taurus.

Helliwell, J., Layard, R. and Sachs, J. (2019) *World Happiness Report 2019* [online], Available from: https://worldhappiness.report/ed/2019/

Hemmings, C. (2005) 'Telling Feminist Stories', *Feminist Theory*, 6(2). https://doi.org/10.1177/1464700105053690

Hemmings, C. (2011) *Why Stories Matter: The Political Grammar of Feminist Theory*. North Carolina: Duke University Press.

Hemmings, C. (2012) 'Affective solidarity: feminist reflexivity and political transformation', *Feminist Theory*, 13(2): 147–61.

Henderson, V.L. (2008) 'Is there hope for anger? The politics of spacializing and (re)producing an emotion', *Emotion, Space and Society*, 1(1): 28–37.

Hill, N., Brinkmann, S. and Peterson, A. (2019) 'Critical happiness studies', in N. Hill, S. Brinkmann and A. Petersen (eds) *Critical Happiness Studies*, London: Routledge.

Hobbs, M., Owen, S. and Gerber, L. (2017) 'Liquid love? Dating apps, sex, relationships and the digital transformation of intimacy', *Journal of Sociology*, 53(2): 271–84.

Hochschild, A.R. (1979) 'Emotion work, feeling rules and social structure', *American Journal of Sociology*, 85(3): 551–75.

Hochschild, A.R. (1983) *The Managed Heart: Commercialization of Human Feeling*, Berkeley, CA: University of California Press.

Hochschild, A.R. (1994) 'The commercial spirit of intimate life and the abduction of feminism: signs from women's advice books', *Theory, Culture and Society*, 11(2): 1–24.

Hochschild, A.R. (1997) *The Time Bind: When Work Becomes Home and Home Becomes Work*, New York: Henry Holt and Company.

Hochschild, A.R. (2003) *The Commercialization of Intimate Life: Notes from Home and Work*, Berkeley: University of California Press.

Hochschild, A.R. (2012) *The Outsourced Self: Intimate Life in Market Times*, New York: Metropolitan Books.

Hochschild, A.R. (2016) *Strangers in their Own Land: Anger and Mourning on the American Right*, New York: New Press.

Holmes, M. (2004) 'The importance of being angry: anger in political life', *European Journal of Social Theory*, 7(2): 123–32.

Holmes, M. (2010) 'The emotionalization of reflexivity', *Sociology*, 44(1): 139–54.

Holmes, M. (2011) 'Introduction: Friendship and Emotions', *Sociological Research Online*, 16(1).

Holmes, M. (2015) 'Men's emotions: Heteromasculinity, emotional reflexivity, and intimate relationships', *Men and Masculinity*, 18: 176–92.

Holmes, M. (2016) *Sociology for Optimists*, London: Sage.

Hooks, B. (1989) *Talking Back: Thinking Feminist, Thinking Black*, Boston: South End Press.

Hookway, N., Barbosa Neves, B., Franklin, A. and Patulny, R. (2019) 'Loneliness and love in late modernity', in R. Patulny, R.E. Olson, S. Khorana, J. McKenzie and R. Peterie (eds) *Emotions in Late Modernity*, London/New York: Routledge, pp 83–97.

Horkheimer, M. and Adorno, T. (1979) [1944] *Dialectic of Enlightenment*, London: Verso.

Hsu, B.Y. and Madsen, R. (2019) *The Chinese Pursuit of Happiness: Anxieties, Hopes and Moral Tensions in Everyday Life*, Berkeley: University of California Press.

Hutchinson, E. (2010) 'Trauma and the politics of emotions: constituting identity, security and community after the Bali bombing', *Internal Relations*, 24(1): 65–86.

Illouz, E. (1997a) *Consuming the Romantic Utopia: Love and the Cultural Contradictions of Capitalism*, Berkeley: University of California Press.

Illouz, E. (1997b) 'Who will care for the caretaker's daughter?: towards a sociology of happiness in the era of reflexive modernity', *Theory, Culture and Society*, 14(4): 31–66.

Illouz, E. (1998) 'The lost innocence of love: romance as a postmodern condition', *Theory, Culture and Society*, 15(3–4): 161–86.

Illouz, E. (2003) *Oprah Winfrey and the Glamour of Misery*, New York: Columbia University Press.

Illouz, E. (2007) *Cold Intimacies: The Making of Emotional Capitalism*, Cambridge: Polity Press.

Illouz, E. (2008) *Saving the Modern Soul: Therapy, Emotions, and the Culture of Self-Help*, Berkeley, CA: University of California Press.

Illouz, E. (2009) 'Emotions, imagination and consumption: a new research agenda', *Journal of Consumer Culture*, 9(3): 377–413.

Illouz, E. (2010) 'Love and its discontents: irony, reason, romance', *The Hedgehog Review*, 12(1): 18–32.

Illouz, E. (2012) *Why Love Hurts: A Sociological Explanation*, London: Polity Press.

Illouz, E. (2014) *Hard-Core Romance: Fifty Shades of Grey, Best Sellers and Society*, Chicago: Chicago University Press.

Illouz, E. (2018) 'Introduction: emodities or the making of emotional commodities', in E. Illouz (ed) *Emotions as Commodities: Capitalism, Consumption and Authenticity*, London: Routledge, pp 1–29.

Illouz, E. and Benger, Y. (2015) 'Emotions and consumption', in D. Cook and J.M. Ryan (eds) *The Wiley Blackwell Encyclopedia of Consumption and Consumer Studies*, London: John Wiley and Sons, pp 263–68.

Illouz, E., Gillon, D. and Shachak, M. (2014) 'Emotions and cultural theory', in J.E. Stets and J.H. Turner (eds) *Handbook of the Sociology of Emotions*, ii, Dordrecht: Springer, pp 221–44.

Jackson, B.A. and Wingfield, A.H. (2013) 'Getting angry to get ahead: Black college men, emotional performance and encouraging respectable masculinity', *Symbolic Interaction*, 36(3): 275–92.

Jacobsen, M.H. (2019) *Emotions, Everyday Life and Sociology*, London: Routledge.

Jacoby, N.R. (2012) 'Grief as a social emotion: theoretical perspectives', *Death Studies*, 36(8): 679–711.

Jaggar, A. (1989) 'Love and knowledge: emotion in feminist epistemology', *Inquiry*, 32(2): 151–76.

Jamieson, l. (1999) 'Intimacy transformed? A critical look at the "pure" relationship', Sociology, 33(3): 477–94.

Jasper, J.M. (2011) 'Emotions and social movements: twenty years of theory and research', *Annual Review of Sociology*, 37: 285–303.

Jonasdottir, A. and Ferguson, A. (eds) (2013) *Love: A Question for Feminism in the Twenty-first Century*, London: Routledge.

Jones, G.W. (2012a) 'Late marriage and low fertility in Singapore: the limits of policy', *The Japanese Journal of Population*, 10: 89–101.

Jones, G.W. (2012b) 'International marriage in Asia: what do we know, and what do we need to know?', Working Paper Series 174, Asia Research Institute, National University of Singapore.

Jones, G.W. and Shen, H. (2008) 'International Marriage in East and Southeast Asia: Trends and Research Emphases', *Citizenship Studies*, 12: 9–25.

Kanai, A. (2015) 'WhatShouldWeCallMe? Self-branding, individuality and belonging in youthful femininities on Tumblr', *M/C Journal*, 18(1). https://doi.org/10.5204/mcj.936

Kanai, A. (2017) 'The best friend, the boyfriend, other girls, hot guys and creeps: the relational production of self on Tumblr', *Feminist Media Studies*, 17(6): 911–25.

Kanai, A. and Gill, R. (2020) 'Woke? Affect, neoliberalism, marginalised identities and consumer culture', *New Formations*, 102: 10–27.

Kane, A. (2001) 'Finding emotion in social movement processes: Irish land movement metaphors and narratives', in J. Goodwin, J.M. Jasper and F. Polletta (eds) *Passionate Politics: Emotions and Social Movements*, Chicago: University of Chicago Press, pp 251–66.

Karppi, T., Kahkonen, L., Manevuo, M., Mari, P. and Sihvonen, T. (2016) 'Affective Capitalism: Investments and Investigations', *ephemera*, 16(4): 1–13.

Kay, K. and Shipman, C. (2014) *The Confidence Code: The Science and Art of Self-Assurance -What Women Should Know,* New York: Harper Collins.
Kelan, E. (2009) *Reforming Gender at Work*, New York: Palgrave, Macmillan.
Keller, J. and Ryan, M. (2014) 'Call for papers: Problematizing Postfeminism', Available from: http://arcyp.ca/archives/4244
Kemper, T.D. (1978) *A Social Interactional Theory of Emotions,* New York: Wiley.
Khanna, R. (2003) *Dark Continent: Psychoanalysis and Colonialism*, Durham: Duke University Press.
King, D.S. (2006) 'Activists and emotional reflexivity: towards Touraine's subject as social movement', *Sociology*, 40(5): 873–91.
Kipnis, L. (2003) *Against Love: A Polemic*, New York: Pantheon.
Kristeva, J. (1982) 'Approaching abjection', in *Powers of Horror*, New York: Columbia University Press, pp 1–31.
Lamont, M. (2012) 'Toward a comparative sociology of valuation and evaluation', *Annual Review of Sociology*, 38(2): 1–21.
Lasch, C. (1977) *Haven in a Heartless World: The Family Besieged*, New York: Basic Books.
Lawler, E.J. (2001) 'An affect theory of social exchange', *American Journal of Sociology*, 107(2): 321–52.
Layder, D. (2004) *Emotion in Social Life*, London: Sage.
Layder, D. (2006) *Understanding Social Theory,* London: Sage.
Lemmings, D. and Brooks, A. (eds) (2014) *Emotions and Social Change: Historical and Sociological Perspectives*, New York: Routledge.
Lenzer, G. (ed) (1983) *Auguste Comte and Positivism: The Essential Writings*, Chicago: University of Chicago Press.
Lively, K. (2008) 'Emotional segues and the management of emotion by women and men', *Social Forces*, 87(2): 911–36.
Lively, K.J. (2019) 'Sociological approaches to the study of gender and emotion in late modernity', in R. Patulny, R.E. Olson, S. Khorana, J. McKenzie, A. Bellocchi and R. Peterie (eds) *Emotions in Late Modernity*, London/New York: Routledge, pp 69–82.
Lively, K.J. and Powell, B. (2006) 'Emotional expression at work and at home: domain, status, or individual characteristics?', *Social Psychology Quarterly*, 69(1): 17–38.
Lively, K.J., Steelman, L.C. and Powell, B. (2006) 'Equity, emotion, and the household division of labour', *Social Psychology Quarterly*, 73(3): 358–79.
Lois, J. (2003) *Heroic Efforts: The Emotional Culture of Search and Rescue Volunteers*, New York: New York University Press.
Lomas, T., Cartwright, T., Edington, T. and Ridge, D. (2016) 'New Ways of being a Man: "Positive" Hegemonic Masculinity in Mediation-based Communities of Practice', *Men and Masculinities*, 19(3): 289–310.

Lopez, C., Hartmann, P. and Apaolaza, V. (2017) 'Gratification on Social Networking Sites: The Role of Secondary School Students' Individual Differences in Loneliness', *Journal of Educational Computing*, 57(4). https://doi.org/10.1177/0735633117743917

Lorde, A. (1984) *Sister Outsider: Essays and Speeches*, Trumansburg: Crossing Press.

Love, H. (2007) 'Compulsory happiness and queer existence', *New Formations,* 63(1).

Luhmann, N. (1986) *Love as Passion*, Stanford: Stanford University Press.

Luhmann, N. (1989) *Ecological Communication*, Cambridge: Polity Press.

Lutz, C. (1988) *Unnatural Emotions*, Chicago: University of Chicago Press.

Mankekar, P. (2021) 'Mobile love: moral panics, erotics and affect', in A. Brooks (ed) *The Routledge Companion to Romantic Love*, London/New York: Routledge, pp 80–96.

Marshall, M. and Witz, A. (2004) *Engendering Social Theory*, London: Sage.

Massumi, B. (2002) *Parable for the Virtual: Movement, Affect, Sensation*, Durham, NC: Duke University Press.

Massumi, B. (2010) 'The future birth of the affective fact: the political ontology of threat', in M. Gregg and G.J. Seigworth (eds) *The Affect Theory Reader*, London: Duke University Press, pp 52–70.

McCracken, G. (1991) *Culture and Consumption: New Approaches to the Symbolic Character of Consumer Goods and Activities*, Bloomington, IN: Indiana University Press.

McKenzie, J. and Patulny, R. (eds) (2022) *Dystopian Emotions*, Bristol: Bristol University Press.

McNess, A. (2008) 'Happy to talk …. To a point: Bereaved young men and emotional disclosure', *Youth Studies Australia*, 27: 25–34.

McRobbie, A. (2009) *The Aftermath of Feminism: Gender, Culture and Social Change*, London: Sage.

McRobbie, A. (2013) 'Feminism, the family and the new "mediated" materialism', *New Formations*, 80–81: 1–26.

McRobbie, A. (2015) 'Notes on the perfect: competitive femininity in neoliberal times', *Australian Feminist Studies*, 30(83): 3–20.

Meagher, M. (2003) 'Jenny Saville and a feminist aesthetics of disgust', *Hypatia*, 18(4): 23–41.

Menninghaus, W. (2003) *Disgust. Theory and History of a Strong Sensation*, New York: SUNY Press.

Montes, V. (2013) 'The role of emotions in the construction of masculinity: Guatemalan migrant men, transnational migration, and family relations', *Gender and Society*, 27(4): 469–90.

Negri, A. (1999) 'Value and affect', *Boundary,* 26(2): 77–88.

Nehring, D., Alvarado, E., Hendricks, E. and Kerrigan, D. (2016) *Transnational Popular Psychology and the Global Self-Help Industry: The Politics of Contemporary Social Change*, New York: Palgrave Macmillan.

Ngai, S. (2005) *Ugly Feelings*, Cambridge, MA, Harvard University Press.

Nolan, J. (1988) *The Therapeutic State: Justifying Government at Century's End*, New York: New York University Press.

Nowotny, H. (1981) 'Women in public life in Austria', in C. Fuchs-Epstein and L.R. Coser (eds) *Access to Power. Cross National Studies of Women and Elites*, London: George, Allen and Unwin.

Nussbaum, M. (2001) *Upheavals of Thought: the Intelligence of Emotions*, Cambridge/New York: Cambridge University Press.

Nussbaum, M.C. (2004) *Hiding from Humanity: Disgust, Shame, and the Law*, Princeton, NJ: Princeton University Press.

Nussbaum, M.C. (2006) *Frontiers of Justice: Disability, Nationality, Species Membership*, Harvard University Press.

O'Neill, R. (2015a) 'Whither Critical Masculinity Studies? Notes on Inclusive Masculinity Theory, Postfeminism, and Sexual Politics', *Men and Masculinities*, 18(1): 100–200.

O'Neill, R. (2015b) 'The work of seduction: Intimacy and subjectivity in the London "seduction community"', *Sociological Research Online*, 20(4): 1–4, Available from LSE Research Online: http://eprints.lse.ac.uk/89849/

O'Neill, R. (2016) 'The aesthetics of sexual discontent: notes from the London "seduction community"', in A. Elias, R. Gill and C. Scharff (eds) *Aesthetic Labour: Rethinking Beauty Politics in Neoliberalism*, London: Palgrave, pp 333–49.

Ong, S.E. (2000) 'Housing affordability and upward mobility from public to private housing in Singapore', *International Real Estate Review*, 3(1): 49–64.

Ouellette, L. (2016) *Lifestyle TV*, New York: Routledge.

Pascoe, C.J. (2007) *Dude You're a Fag: Masculinity and Sexuality in High School*, Berkeley: University of California Press.

Patulny, R. and Olson, R.E. (2019) 'Emotions in Late Modernity', in R. Patulny, R.E. Olson, S. Khorana, J. McKenzie, A. Bellocchi and R. Peterie (eds) *Emotions in Late Modernity*, London/New York: Routledge, pp 8–24.

Patulny, R. and Wong, M. (2012) 'Poor mothers and lonely single males. The "essentially" excluded women and men of Australia', *Social Policy and Society*, 12(2): 221–39.

Patulny, R., Olson, R.E., Khorana, S., McKenzie, J., Bellocchi, A., Peterie, M. (2019) 'Introduction', in R. Patulny, R.E. Olson, S. Khorana, J. McKenzie, A. Bellocchi and R. Peterie (eds) *Emotions in Late Modernity*, London/New York: Routledge.

Pease, B. (2012) 'The politics of gendered emotions: disrupting men's emotional investment in privilege', *Australian Journal of Social Issues*, 47(1): 125–42.

Pedwell, C. and Whitehead, A. (2012) 'Affecting feminism: questions of feeling in feminist theory', *Feminist Theory*, 13(2): 115–29.

Perez-Alvarez, M. (2012) 'Positive psychology: sympathetic magic', *Papeles Del Psicologo*, 33(3): 183–201.

Pierce, J.L. (1995) *Gender Trials: Emotional Lives in Contemporary Law Firms*, Berkeley, CA: University of California Press.

Poder, P. (2008) 'Bauman on freedom – consumer freedom as the integration mechanism of liquid society', in M.H. Jacobsen and P. Poder (eds) *The Sociology of Zygmunt Bauman: Challenges and Critiques*, Hampshire: Ashgate, pp 97–115.

Powell, J. and Gilbert, T. (2008) 'Social theory and emotion: sociological excursions', *International Journal of Sociology and Social Policy*, 28(9/10): 394–407.

Probyn, E. (2000) *Carnal Appetites. Food Sex Identities*, New York: Routledge.

Probyn, E. (2004) 'Everyday shame', *Cultural Studies*, 18(2–3): 328–49.

Probyn, E. (2005) *Blush: Faces of Shame*, Minneapolis: University of Minnesota Press.

Qu, L. (2020) 'Households and families', *Australian Institute of Family Studies Report*, 1–14.

Reay, D. (2004) 'Gendering Bourdieu's concept of capital: emotional capital, women and social class', *Sociological Review*, 52(2): 57–74.

Reay, D. (2005) 'Beyond consciousness? The psychic landscape of social class', *Sociology*, 39(5): 911–28.

Reddy, W. (2001) *The Navigation of Feeling: A Framework for the History of Emotions*, New York: Cambridge University Press.

Richardson, D. (2010) 'Youth masculinities: compelling male heterosexuality', *The British Journal of Sociology*, 61: 737–56.

Ritzer, G. (2004) *The Globalization of Nothing*, Thousand Oaks, CA: Pine Forge Press.

Roberts, S. (2013) 'Boys will be boys…. won't they? Change and continuities in contemporary young working-class masculinities', *Sociology*, 47(4): 671–86.

Roberts, S. (ed) (2015) *Debating Modern Masculinities: Change, Continuity, Crisis*, London: Palgrave, Macmillan.

Rottenberg, C. (2014a) 'The rise of neoliberal feminism', *Cultural Studies*, 28(3): 418–37.

Rottenberg, C. (2014b) 'Happiness and the liberal imagination: how superwoman became balanced', *Feminist Studies*, 40(1): 144–68.

Sandberg, S. (2013) *Lean In: Women, Work and the Will to Lead*, New York: W.H. Allen.

Scheff, T.J. (1966) *Being Mentally Ill: A Sociological Theory*, New York: Routledge.

Scheff, T.J. (1974) 'The labelling theory of mental illness', *American Sociological Review*, 39(3): 444–52.

Scheff, T.J. (1990) *Microsociology: Discourse, Emotion and Social Structure*, Chicago: University of Chicago Press.

Scheff, T.J. (2012) 'A social/emotional theory of "mental illness"', *International Journal of Social Psychiatry*, 59(1): 87–92.

Schieman, S. (2006) 'Anger', in J.E. Stets and J.H. Turner (eds) *Handbook of the Sociology of Emotions*, New York: Springer, pp 493–515.

Schnittker, J. (2008) 'Diagnosing our national disease: trends in income and happiness, 1973–2004', *Social Psychology Quarterly*, 71(3): 257–80.

Schrock, D.P., Boyd, E.M. and Leaf, M. (2009) 'Emotion work in the public performance of male-to-female transsexuals', *Archives of Sexual Behaviour*, 38(5): 702–12.

Sedgwick, E.K. (2003) *Touching Feeling: Affect, Pedagogy, Performativity*, North Carolina: Duke University Press.

Seidler, V.J. (1994) *Unreasonable Men: Masculinity and Social Theory*, London: Routledge.

Sennett, R. (1998) *The Corrosion of Character. The Personal Consequences of Work in the New Capitalism*, New York: W.W. Norton and Company.

Shepherd, C.K. (2015) 'The role of women in international conflict resolution', *Journal of Public Law and Policy*, 36(2): Article 1.

Shields, S.A. (2002) *Speaking from the Heart: Gender and the Social Meaning of Emotion*, Cambridge: Cambridge University Press.

Shumway, D. (2003) *Modern Love: Romance, Intimacy and the Marriage Crisis*, New York: New York University Press.

Shumway, D. (2022) 'What's love got to do with it? Romance and intimacy in an age of hooking up', in A. Brooks (ed) *The Routledge Companion to Romantic Love*, London/New York: Routledge.

Simmel, G. (2004) [1903] 'The metropolis and mental life', in M. Malcolm (ed) *The City Cultures Reader*, London: Routledge.

Simon, R.W. and Nath, L.E. (2004) 'Gender and emotion in the United States: do men and women differ in self-reports of feelings and expressive behaviour?' *American Journal of Sociology*, 109(5): 1137–76.

Simon, R.W. and Lively, K. (2010) 'Sex, anger and depression', *Social Forces*, 88(4): 1543–68.

Skeggs, B. (1997) *Formations of Class and Gender: Becoming Respectable*, London: Sage.

Skeggs, B. (2005) 'The making of class and gender through visualizing moral subject formation', *Sociology*, 39(5): 965–82.

Skeggs, B. (2009) 'The moral economy of person production: the class relations of self-performance on "reality" television', *Sociological Review*, 57(4): 626–44.

Skeggs, B. (2010) 'The value of relationships: affective scenes and emotional performances', *Feminist Legal Studies*, 18(1): 29–51.

Slaughter, A-M. (2015) *Unfinished Business*, London: Oneworld Publications.

Smart, C. (2007) *Personal Life*, Cambridge: Polity Press.

Smart, C., Neale, B. and Wade, A. (2001) *The Changing Experience of Childhood, Families and Divorce*, London: Polity Press.

Smelser, N.J. (1998) 'The rational and the ambivalent in the social sciences: 1997 presidential address', *American Sociological Review*, 63(1): 1–16.

Spelman, E. (1989) *Inessential Woman: Problems of Exclusion in Feminist Thought*, Boston: Beacon Press.

Stanley, M., Moyle, W., Ballantyne, A., Jaworski, K., Corlis, M., Oxlade, D., Stoll, A. and Young, B. (2010) 'Nowadays, you don't even see your neighbours: loneliness in the everyday lives of older Australians', *Health and Social Care in the Community*, 18(4): 407–14.

Stearns, P.N. and Lewis, J. (1998) *An Emotional History of the United States*, New York: New York University Press.

Stearns, C.Z. and Stearns, P.N. (1986) *Anger: The Struggle for Emotional Control in America's History*, Chicago: University of Chicago Press.

Stets, J.E. (2012) 'Current emotions research in sociology: advances in the discipline', *Emotion Review*, 4(3): 326–32.

Stone, L. (1997) *The Family, Sex and Marriage in England, 1500–1800*, New York: Harper and Row.

Storr, M. (2002) 'Classy lingerie', *Feminist Review*, 71(1): 18–36, Available from: https://doi-org.ezproxy2.acu.au/10.1057/palgrave.fr9400032

Strijbosch, K. (2015) 'Single and the city: state influences on intimate relationships of young, single, well-educated women in Singapore', *Journal of Marriage and Family*, 77(5): 1108–25.

Swidler, A. (2001) *Talk of Love: How Culture Matters*, Chicago: University of Chicago Press.

Sydie, R. (2004) 'Feminist Sociology: Past and Present Challenges', in N. Genov (ed) *Advances in Sociological Knowledge: Over Half a Century*, Wiesbaden: Springer.

Tan, H. and Forgas, J. (2010) 'When happiness makes us selfish, but sadness makes it fair: Affective influences on interpersonal strategies in the Dictator Game', *Journal of Experimental Social Psychology*, 46(3): 571–76.

Tasker, Y. and Negra, D. (2007) *Interrogating Postfeminism: Gender and the Politics of Popular Culture*, North Carolina: Duke University Press.

Taylor, C. (2007) *A Secular Age*, Cambridge: Harvard University Press.

Thien, D. (2005) 'After and beyond feeling? A consideration of affect and emotion in geography', *Area*, 37(4): 450–6.

Thoits, P.A. (2004) 'Emotion norms, emotion work and social order', in A.S.R. Manstead, N. Frijda and A. Fischer (eds) *Feelings and Emotions: The Amsterdam Symposium*, Cambridge: Cambridge University Press.

Thompson, N. (1997) 'Masculinity and Loss', in D. Field, J. Hockney and N. Small (eds) *Death, Gender and Ethnicity*, London: Routledge.

Thompson, L. and Donaghue, N. (2014) 'The confidence trick. Competing constructions of confidence and self-esteem in young Australian women's discussions of the sexualization of culture', *Women's Studies International Forum,* 47: 23–35.

Turkle, S. (2011/2013) *Alone Together: Why we Expect More from Technology and Less from Each Other,* New York: Basic Books.

Turkle, S. (2015) *Reclaiming Conversation,* New York: Penguin.

Turner, B. (1998) Review of Eva Illouz, *Consuming the Romantic Utopia: Love and the Cultural Contradictions of Capitalism,* in *Body and Society,* 43(3): 115–20.

Turner, B. (2018) '(I can't get no) satisfaction: happiness and successful societies', *Sociology,* 54(3): 279–93.

Turner, J.H. (2005) 'Conceptualizing emotions sociologically', in J.H. Turner and J.E. Stets (eds) *The Sociology of Emotions,* Cambridge: Cambridge University Press, pp 1–25.

Turner, J. (2009) 'The sociology of emotions: basic theoretical arguments', *Emotion Review,* 1(4): 340–54.

Turner, J.H. and Stets, J.E. (eds) (2005) *The Sociology of Emotions,* Cambridge: Cambridge University Press.

Turner, J.H. and Stets, J.E. (2006) *Handbook of the Sociology of Emotions,* New York: Springer.

Tyler, I. (2013) *Revolting Subjects: Social Abjection and Resistance in Neoliberal Britain,* London: Bloomsbury Academic and Professional.

Tyler, I. and Gill, R. (2013) 'Postcolonial girl: mediated intimacy and migrant audibility', *Interventions: International Journal of Postcolonial Studies,* 15(1): 78–94.

Valenti, J. (2014a) 'When everyone is a feminist is anyone?', *The Guardian,* [online] 24 November, Available from: http://www.theguardian.com/commentisfree/2014/nov/24/when-everyone-is-a-feminist

Valenti, J. (2014b) 'The female "confidence gap" is sham', *The Guardian,* [online] 23 April, Available from: https://www.theguardian.com/commentisfree/2014/apr/23/female-confidence-gap-katty-kay-claire-shipman

Weber, M. (1978) *Economy and Society: An Outline of Interpretive Sociology,* trans. Guenther Roth et al, Berkeley, CA: University of California Press.

Weber, B.R. (2009) *Makeover TV. Selfhood, Citizenship and Celebrity,* Durham, NC: Duke University Press.

Welcomer, S.A., Dennis, A. and Kilduff (2000) 'Resisting the Discourse of Modernity: Rationality Versus Emotion in Hazardous Waste Siting', *Human Relations,* 53(9): 1175–205.

Wharton, A.S. (2009) 'The sociology of emotional labour', *Annual Review of Sociology,* 35: 147–65.

Wilson, A. (2010) 'Post-Fordist desires: the commodity aesthetics of Bangkok sex shows', *Feminist Legal Studies,* 18(1): 53–67.

Wilson, E. (1985) *Adorned in Dreams: Fashion and Modernity,* London: Virago.

Wong, T. and Yeoh, B. (2003) 'Fertility and the family: an overview of pro-natalist population policies in Singapore', Asian MetaCentre Research Paper Series No 12, Available from: http://www.populationasia.org/Publications/RP/AMCRP12.pdf

Wouters, C. (1989) 'The sociology of emotions and flight attendants: Hochschild's managed heart', *Theory, Culture and Society*, 6(1): 95–123.

Wouters, C. (1991) 'On status competition and emotion management', *Journal of Social History*, 29(2): 325–39.

Wouters, C. (1995) 'Etiquette books and emotion management in the 20th century: Part two- the integration of the sexes', *Journal of Social History*, 29(2): 325–39.

Wouters, C. (2007) *Informalization: Manners and Emotions since 1890*, London: Sage Publications.

Wright, K. (2011) *The Rise of Therapeutic Culture: Psychological Knowledge and the Contradictions of Cultural Change*, Washington, DC: New Academic Publishing.

Yang, Y. (2008) 'Social inequalities in happiness in the United States, 1972–2004: an age-period cohort analysis', *American Sociological Review*, 73(2): 204–26.

Yeatman, A. (1994) *Postmodern Revisionings of the Political*, London/New York: Routledge.

Yeoh, B., Leng, G.H.D. and Dung, V.T. (2013) 'Commercially arranged marriage and the negotiation of citizenship rights among Vietnamese marriage migrants in multiracial Singapore', *Asian Ethnicity*, 14(2): 139–56.

Zinn, J.O. (2006) 'Risk, affect and emotion', *Forum: Qualitative Social Research*, 7(1): 1–9.

# Index

## A

abjection 76
Aboriginal and non-Aboriginal cultures 74
abuse 47, 63
activism, left-wing and civil rights 48
actor, premodern 85
advantage and disadvantage 90
advice books and magazines 81, 89
affairs, self-contained 83
affect and affect studies 6, 9, 13, 16–18, 21, 22, 24, 39, 40, 41, 45, 47, 55, 60, 64, 71, 72, 74
affective and psychic life 45
affective contagion 43
affective dissonance 41
affective faculties 22
affective investments 38
affective judgement 67
affective neutrality 21, 33
affective solidarity 41
affective spaces 62
affective turn 17–18, 22–6, 38–40
age and age limitation 11–12, 86, 92
agency and agents 27, 34, 44, 61, 64, 91
alienation 13, 14, 21
alternative futures 70–1
ambiguity 32
  of capitalism, identity and art 56
  of privacy, intimacy and sexuality 56
ambition 62
ambivalence 32, 35, 37, 70, 71
anger 4, 8, 10–11, 29, 33, 34, 45, 54, 64, 67, 71, 73–4, 85
anti-foundationalist movements 43
anxiety 27, 32, 35, 71
associative life 82
atomising 31
attachments, strong 85
attraction 85
attribution 23
authority, traditional forms of 30, 31
autonomy 30, 87
aversive emotions 76 *see also* disgust

## B

beauty industry 45, 64
behaviour, organizing, structuring and regulation of 13, 21, 23
biography, romantic individual 82, 83
birth and fertility rates 91
body
  love campaigns 63
  –mind dichotomy 16–17, 75
  shame and 74
bonds and bonding 14, 36, 85
boredom 32
boundaries, blurring of 84
brain chemistry 85

## C

calling 87, 88
capital and capitalism 7, 16, 18–19, 20, 21, 24, 28, 54, 56, 58, 59, 60–6, 69, 72, 80, 81, 82–8, 92 *see also* neoliberal capitalism
care 28
change and transformation 26, 27–8, 31, 35–6, 43, 49, 50, 62, 64, 65–6, 71, 88, 89
chick-lit genre 84
children and childhood 35, 86
choice making 27, 28, 31, 43, 57, 70, 85, 87, 88, 89
civilization and the civilizing process 21, 31, 70
class 7, 10, 14, 31, 33, 35, 54–6, 66, 73, 78
classical age 31
closeness 81
cognitivism 13
collective angst 71
collective social and moral order, maintaining 31
collectivity, injury to 76
comfort 81
commercialization 23, 28, 66
commitment 35
commodities and commodification 44, 56, 57, 60, 82
community and togetherness 30, 41, 75

companionship and companionate marriage 36, 79
compassion 74–5
compatibility, criteria adopted to establish 85–6
competition 31, 90
complaint 64
condensation 25
confidence 15, 44, 46, 47, 49, 58, 60–3
culture 7, 39, 46, 53, 59, 60–6
conformity and acquiescence 70
connections, replacement of relationships by 36
consciousness and consciousness-raising strategy 27, 48, 63, 76
consumer
  capitalism 18, 59 *see also* capital and capitalism
  conceptualization of as emotional entity 59
  culture, growth of 59
  market 31, 44, 57–8, 59, 65, 81, 82, 85–6, 87, 88, 90
  needs 59
  sphere, formation of 59
consumers and consumerism 25, 32, 35, 44, 57, 82, 88, 90, 92
consumption 17, 18–19, 25, 31–2, 49, 56–60, 70, 83 *see also* postfeminism
contact, resumption of 88
contemporary masculinities scholarship 50
contemporary social theory and the affective turn 22–6
context, social and cultural 27, 90, 91
contingency 80–1
control
  individual 31
  of romantic encounters and marriage 87–8, 89, 92
conventions of expression and performativity 39
conversation, internal 27
corporate culture 61
costs of emotion management 24
courtly love 78–9
courtship process 87
cover stories 81
COVID-19, impact of on emotions 71
critical masculinity studies 47, 49
cultural and social expression 42
cultural capital 7, 53, 58, 66
cultural constructs 48, 75
cultural cooling 81
cultural discourses 83
cultural history of love 86
cultural ideal 35
cultural influence 44–5
cultural life, contemporary 45
cultural movement 86, 87
cultural norms 34
cultural representation 25
cultural standards 15–16
cultural status and expectations of love 82–3, 85
cultural theory 82
cultural trauma 76
culture 13
  contemporary 45
  neoliberal 61, 89
  popular 68

**D**

daily life, emotional demands and contingencies of 25
dancing 88
dangerous bodies 67
de-emotionalization 71
deliberation 27
democracy in the public sphere 30
democratic bargaining 90
democratizing of interpersonal relationships 30
demoralization 86
depression, men's underreporting of 48
deregulation 44, 87, 88
desexualisation of women's bodies 44
desire 25, 83, 89, 92–3
  consumption and 57
  to leave partner 35
  object of 79
  post-Fordist 55–6
desires, individualistic and sexual 22
destabilization 35
detachment 55, 71
detraditionalization 27, 81
devotion 54
digital communication and relationships 31, 32, 36
discipline 43, 44, 45, 64
discourse and discourse studies 25, 49, 68, 72, 79, 80, 83, 89–90
discursive formations and repertoires 61, 89
disenchantment of the world 71
disenfranchised populations 76
disgust 43, 76–7
dislocation 32
disorder 70, 71
distress 33–4, 71
divorce 22
domestic and caring responsibilities and labour 62, 81
domestic idealism 74
domination 62, 68
Dopamine 85
dramaturgical perspective 23
drugs and relationship states 85
dysfunctionality 22
dystopia 70

**E**

economic and class-based enterprise 78
economic power and redistribution 65, 86

# INDEX

economics, happiness 68
economization of social relationships 87
education 85, 92
effervescence 13
efficiency 89
Elysian school 23
embodiment 49
emodity 59
emotion
  cultural and structural theories of 13, 33, 42–3
  rationality and gender 14, 15, 22, 33, 40
  work 13, 14, 23, 28, 40, 48, 81
emotional arousal 13
emotional authenticity 60, 88
emotional autonomy 87
emotional branding 59
emotional capital 5, 53, 92
  and emotional commodities 7, 53–66
  and social class, traditional conceptions of 54–6, 66
emotional capitalism 46, 66, 70
emotional change 60
emotional commitment to ideas and social practices 25
emotional competence 55
emotional complexity in late modernity 5–6, 29–37
emotional consciousness 21
emotional economy 16
emotional engagement, diminished 71
emotional expressiveness 58
emotional fulfilment 19, 58, 81, 89
emotional habitus 16
emotional inexpressivity in men 38
emotional intelligence 24
emotional intersections 6–7, 38–52
emotional intimacy 88 *see also* intimacy
emotional labour 14, 23, 24, 28, 33, 40, 41, 54, 60
emotional life 41, 87
emotional make-up 60
emotional management strategies 14, 23, 33
emotional options 55
emotional/rational divide 29
emotional response 75
emotional satisfaction 58
emotional standards and norms for men and women 32–3
emotional tension 35
emotionality 20, 58
emotionalization of reflexivity 27–8, 30
emotions
  and affect 16–18, 39, 41–2 *see also* affect and affect studies
  analysis of 2
  aversive 76 *see also* anger; disgust; fear; shame
  in classical sociological theories 20–2
  and cognition 21, 57
  collectivized and individualized–privatized 29
  commodification of 18, 24, 32, 56–60, 92
  complex 34–6
  concepts and perspectives on 1, 4–5, 9–19
  consumption and commodities 56–60
  control of 21, 22, 23
  cultural perspectives on 5, 9, 15–16, 25, 33, 57, 75
  distinction between background and situational 57
  and economy 58 *see also* capital and capitalism; commercialization; commodities and commodification
  feminism and the 4–5, 6, 9, 16–19, 38–47
  gender in 6–7, 23, 24, 25, 29, 38–52, 54, 55–6
  history of 5, 15–16, 20–8
  individualized and collectivized 31, 32
  interpretation of 31
  language of 3, 4–5, 9–19
  legitimacy of 73
  love and intimacy 8, 25, 28, 57, 78–93
  management of 25
  masculinities and 6, 38, 47–52
  mediated 32
  modern 31
  in modernity 5, 20–8
  multidisciplinary nature of 1, 2–3
  new 32
  objectification of 60
  organization of 88
  politics and trauma 74–6
  positive and negative 7–8, 46–7, 59, 67–77 *see also* love; lust; optimism; self-confidence
  and power 23, 40, 78, 86
  primary 10
  privatized 5–6, 29–37
  and rationality 16–17, 31–2
  regime of performativity of 88
  secondary 10
  self-reproach 31, 32 *see also* guilt; shame
  shaping of by social conditions 28
  social class and 14, 33, 54–6, 66
  socially desirable properties of 48
  sociological perspectives on 5, 9–10, 12–15, 25, 28, 34, 76, 82, 87
  theorizing of 1–2
  typology of 10
  *see also different emotions, e.g.* happiness; reflexivity, emotions and identity
empowerment 43, 44, 80
enchanted version of love and intimacy 81, 84
energy 39
Enlightenment
  modernity 21, 22

philosophy 20, 68, 69
project 68
enterprise and entrepreneurial spirit 44, 65, 89, 90
environments, corporate and economic 60
equality 45, 61, 86, 90–1
erotic/passionate love and attractiveness 79, 88
Estrogen *see* Oestrogen
ethics, everyday 73, 74
ethnographic research 49
exchange 28, 55
exclusion of certain groups and persons 76–7
experiences 40, 48, 74–5, 80, 81, 82, 83, 84, 87
external material rewards and developments 32, 82

**F**
fairness, ideal of 86
family and home 10, 11, 34, 42, 74, 80, 82, 85, 87, 91, 93
fashion and fashion industry 45, 56
fear 10, 14–15, 27, 34, 71
feeling
  and affect 39
  in developing marketing strategies 24
  negotiation and experience of 40
  rules 13, 23, 24, 28, 56, 60, 73, 81
  structures of 66
  subject 13
feelings 66, 75, 86
  management of 40, 57
  political aspects of 64
  ugly 42, 76 *see also* disgust; hatred and dislike
female, primitive and embodied 21
female autonomy 87
feminine
  ideal 90
  mystique, debunking of notion of 86
feminism 90
  contemporary 60
  and cultural theory and history 7, 86, 88
  epistemological break within 43
  hegemonic Anglo-American 43
  hijacking of 81
  inclusivity of 45, 64
  individualization of 65
  luminosity of 45, 63
  and neoliberalism 39, 40, 64, 65–6
  pastness of 43–4
  political underpinnings of 65
  popular vs academic 43, 62–4
  remaking of 39, 64, 65
  renouncement of 62
  second-wave 43, 60, 65
  transformative nature of 64, 65–6
  visibility of 45, 63

feminist approach 38
feminist culture wars 60
feminist discourse 46, 65–6, 83
feminist identities 45
feminist intervention, political models of 61
feminist knowledge and affect 41
feminist movement 86
feminist perspectives
  contemporary 43–7, 49
  early 47, 49
feminist theory and theorizing 25, 82 *see also* feminism
feminist turn 61
flexibility 80–1
flight attendants, recruitment and training of 23, 24
fluidity 31
forgiveness 70
free markets and trade 44 *see also* market *under* consumer
freedom 30, 31
friends and friendship 79, 88
frustration 33
fulfilment, long-term 68
functionalist theorists 22

**G**
gay liberation 83
gender 50, 89
  and class, intersection of 7, 53
  differences 11, 54
  and emotion, intersection of 14, 15, 22, 33, 40
  and race 33
  and social class 33
  and social structure 34
  women and anger 33–4
  *see also* gender in *under* emotions
gender and emotional complexity 29
  in late modernity 32–4
gender binary, traditional 33, 34
gender diversity in the workplace 61
gender equality 61, 90–1
gender inequalities 48, 49, 62, 65, 81
gendered assumptions arising in organizational contexts 23
gendered capital 54
gendered nature of emotions and emotional labour 23, 24, 25, 55–6
gendered neoliberalism 45–6
gendered power relations 47, 49, 50, 51, 52
General Social Survey 33
generosity 54
global transformation and globalization 26, 80
globalized neoliberalism and technology 31
goods, emotional and symbolic nature of 58, 59
governability and government 25, 92

# INDEX

grief 48, 76
gross national happiness (GNH) index 69
gross national product (GNP) 69
group consciousness 76
guilt 12, 32

## H

habitus 16, 25, 74
happiness 4, 45
  and age 11–12
  economics 68
  fantasy of 72
  gospel of 68
  indicator *see* marriage
  industry 32, 72
  love as source of all 86
  science of 68, 72
  studies, critical perspectives on 7–8, 11, 67–72
  turn 68, 72
hatred and dislike 75
healing and recovery 61
hegemonic masculinities 48–9, 50
hegemony 13, 25
heteronormativity 51
heterosexism 51
heterosexual men and relationships 48, 51, 62, 72, 87, 88–93 *see also* in heterosexual relationships *under* women
hierarchies, social and political 40, 84, 88
homohysteria, cultural 49–51
homophobia 50–1
honour 73
hook-ups 81
hope and pessimism 70 *see also* optimism
hormones 85
hostility, reduction of 70
households and government-subsidized housing 71, 92
human advancement 44
hurt 86

## I

identity and identities 12, 26, 31, 35, 64, 65, 76, 82, 84, 86
Illouz, Eva 15–16, 35, 46, 55, 56–7, 58–60, 66, 68, 82–8, 90
image-based social media 36 *see also* media industries and advertising
immediacy 36
imperative 46
impression 18, 75
inclusive masculinity theory 6, 47, 49–50, 51
income, rise in 11, 86
indignation 64
individual
  responsibility 31
  victims and collectivities 75

individuality and individualism 25, 26, 30, 35, 43, 44, 46, 64, 90
individualization 26, 29, 30, 71–2, 80–1, 87
individuals and state 82, 91, 92
industry, happiness 32, 72
inequality 34, 46, 48, 49, 62, 65, 76, 81
infatuation 83, 85
inferiority and lack of self-worth 63
injustice 73
innate, expression of 75
insecurity 25, 35, 45, 46, 47, 63
instrumentalist values 82
intellect and intellectual 22, 74
intensities 39, 83
interaction order and patterns of interactionism 23, 30
interest 74
interior life, makeover of 45
interiority 39
internet technology and loneliness 36, 85–6
interpellation 25
interpretive processes 23
interrogation, intersectional 46
intervention, how sociology of emotions operates as 24, 25
intimacy
  and class 55, 56
  detraditionalization of 81
  ideal of 82
  individualized nature of 80, 89
  and love 32, 34–6, 80, 81, 82
  mediated in heterosexual men 88–93
  new 30
  provision of by image-based social media 36
intimate bonds and relationships 29, 35, 36, 80–1, 86, 88, 89, 91
intimate entrepreneurships 89
intimate life 28, 81
intimate public sphere 42
investment 89
irony, trope of 84
irritation 33

## J

joyfulness 70

## K

knowledge
  about interface between ontological and epistemic considerations 41
  expert 60
  feminist concern between affect, power and 17, 18, 41
  and intellect, focus on in descriptions of shame 74
  modern scientific 21
  systems, objectification of emotions through 60
  *see also* psychological research and knowledge

knowledges, production of novel technology of self by set of 61

## L

labelling theory 14, 23
labour 11, 89
language and linguistics 39, 41, 43, 68, 70–1
late capitalism 80
late modern era 30–1
late modernity
    emotional and relational complexity in 5–6, 29–37
    growth of psy-industries in 60
    individualization and society in 26, 71–2, 80–1
    love and intimacy in 34–6, 81
    shift from modernity to 34
    vulnerability of the self in 87
law, marital 79
liberal state 82
lifestyles 87
liminality, institutionalization of 84
lingerie, private and public world of 56
logics 81, 85–6, 90
loneliness 29, 32, 34–6, 71–2, 85–6
loss 48
love 39, 48, 72
    and capitalism 82–8
    confluent 80
    and consumerism 82
    cool modern 81
    cultural status and expectations of 82–3, 85
    distressing nature of 86
    enchanted and disenchanted approach to 81, 84, 85
    as epiphenomenon 85
    falling in 85
    at first sight 82–3, 84
    heterosexual romantic 87
    importance of in marriage 87
    internal 32
    and intimacy 32, 34–6, 80, 81, 82
    lifelong narrative of 83
    liquid 35
    practice of 82
    rules of 81, 86
    soul-mate 36
    as source of all happiness 86
    transformation of 82, 88
love bonds 35, 57
lust 32, 83, 85

## M

*Madame Bovary* (Flaubert) 83
makeover paradigm 44, 45, 64
male chivalry, debunking of notion of 86
male dominance 45, 86
management and enterprise 23, 24, 44, 65, 89, 90
manners 15, 30, 31, 80
marginalized communities and groups 76, 77
marital intimacy 79–80
marriage 22, 72, 78, 79–80, 87, 88, 91–2
Marx and Marxism 13, 21, 23
masculinities 22, 62, 89–90 *see also* inclusive masculinity theory; masculinities and *under* emotions
mass media 36, 86, 89, 90
material rewards, developments and issues 32, 62, 82
maturity 12
Maui, fires on 75, 76
meaning, loss of 71
media industries and advertising 36, 86, 89, 90
medieval manuals of manners 15, 30, 80
memory 76
men
    emotionally expressive 48
    -ology 89
    practices and responses of 51, 90
    repression of emotions by 48
    wellbeing and health of 49
mental and emotional health and well-being 7, 48, 60, 68
mental illness 14
middle class 61, 65–6, 82, 87, 88
migration 67, 75
minority groups 73
misery 56
modernity
    darkness of 71
    and happiness 69, 70
    liquid 30–1, 71
    and love 86
    shift from to late modernity 34
modernization theory 27, 36, 81
monitoring 43, 44, 45
moral constraints 21
moral duty 22
mortality 48
motivation 49
mutual support and commonality 30, 41, 75

## N

narrative 90
nature, control of 21
neediness, repudiation of 46, 47
negotiation 40, 80–1
neoliberal capitalism 9, 18, 46, 48–9, 60–6, 89, 90
neoliberal culture 61, 89
neoliberal feminism 64, 65–6
neoliberal ideology 69–70, 77, 90
neoliberal terms and values 30, 62, 69–70
neoliberalism 7, 17, 25, 30, 31, 39, 40, 44, 45–6, 65, 77, 89
neo-utilitarian politics 70

# INDEX

neuroscience 85
non-conscious 27
Norepinephrine 85
norms and normlessness 18, 21, 23, 28, 31, 32–3, 38, 45, 56, 72, 84, 88
novelty 27

## O

objectification 44
objective circumstances 27
Oedipal conflict 85
Oestrogen 85
online dating 86
ontological and epistemological, entrance into 41
ontological insecurity and risk 25
openness 31, 37, 81
optimism 49, 50, 72
organizational management 23, 24
Oxytocin 85

## P

pain 48, 68, 87
parents and parenting 81, 87, 88
partner selection and improvement 85–6, 87, 88
passion and passionate love 41, 79, 87
patriarchal frameworks, impact of emotions on neoliberal-capitalist 48–9
patriarchy 25, 42, 45, 48, 64
personal and public, intersection of 42, 73
personal life and emotional fulfilment 19, 81, 89
personality, interaction between individual and social structure 23
physical well-being 68
physiological events 28
pick-up and pick-up training 90
planning and strategy 61, 71, 89–90
pleasure 35, 41, 68, 83
political affiliation 85
political behaviour and response 73, 75
political economy 24, 44
political ideology 69, 70
politics and war, intersection of emotions with 8, 75, 77 *see also* sexual politics
populist celebrations 46
positive mental attitude and psychology 44, 45, 46, 63, 68, 70, 71
positivity vs negativity 64–5, 74
postcolonial milieu 74
postfeminism 18, 39, 43–4, 45–6, 47, 49, 51–2, 62, 64, 89
postmodernism 25, 83, 84
postmodernity 30–1, 39, 71, 80
power 6, 14, 46, 76
  affect and 40
  convergence between economic and sexual 86

deterritorialization of patriarchal 64
and emotions 23, 40, 78, 86
and prestige 15
psychic life of 61, 86
relations and structures of 17, 47, 49, 50, 51, 52, 56, 70, 76, 80, 86
and status 14
practical and symbolic work 54
precarity 31
premodern actor 85
pride 14, 34
private life and sphere 24, 42, 54, 56, 60, 73, 74, 82
privatization 44
privileged site 84
professionalism and professions 33, 86
proletariat, suffering and deprivation of the 13
psy-sciences and industries 7, 60, 61, 68, 80, 84–5, 86
psyche 45, 61, 75, 86
psychic disorders and trauma 85, 86
psychoanalysis and psychoanalysts 85, 86
psychological research and knowledge 13, 80, 85–6, 88
public and private self, dichotomy between 24, 42, 56, 73
public sphere 65–6, 71, 74
pure relations and relationships 32, 36, 37, 80–1, 83, 87, 90

## Q

qualitative empirical data, analysis of 82
queer unhappiness 72

## R

race 33, 46, 56, 61, 63, 64
rage 41
rationality and rationalization 20, 21, 40, 44, 58, 65, 69, 70, 71, 84, 85, 86, 87, 89, 90
realities, apocalyptic 70–1
reason 83, 84
  /emotion binary 40
  *see also* rationality and rationalization
reciprocity, ideal of 86
recognition 65
reconciliation 42, 80
reflexive analysis 34
reflexive consciousness 27
reflexive modernization 27, 36
reflexivity, emotions and identity 26–8, 30, 80, 86
regulation of individual behaviour 21
relational complexity 29
  in late modernity 29–32
relational construction 26
relational feedback loops 14
relationship break-up, high risk of 27
relationship manuals 30, 80

relationships
  characterized by strong attachments 85
  exchange 55
  expressiveness of men within 48
  fragility of 35
  intensification of 60
  intimate 29, 35, 36, 80–1, 88, 89, 91
  liberation from traditional conceptions of 29, 31, 80
  long-term committed and lifelong 35, 36, 81, 85
  modern 88
  of obligation and responsibility 55
  of power 17, 47, 49, 50, 51, 52, 56, 70, 80, 86
  pure 32, 36, 37, 80–1, 83, 87, 90
  short-term/temporary nature of 32, 36, 71
  sustaining of 81
  tragic in 83
religion
  centrality of to rituals of interaction 21
  origins of 13
repetition compulsion 85
representational patterns 89
resilience 44
resources 41, 54, 55
restlessness 35
restraint, effective 21
risk and reward 25, 27, 32, 35, 62, 71, 82
ritual patterns and ritualized actions 21, 87, 88
romance
  and marriage 79
  as a postmodern condition 82–8
romantic love 35
  and the emergence of intimacy 57, 78–81
  tradition of 82–3, 87–8
romantic narratives 78–9, 80, 81
romantic objectives and practices 86, 90
romanticization of commodities 82
routine action 27
rules of conduct 81, 86 see also rules under feeling

**S**

sacred objects 21
sanctions 73
scholarship 90
science
  of happiness 68, 72
  and scientific knowledge and interest 21, 31
second-wave feminist analysis see affect studies; affective turn
seduction community 89, 90
self 23, 85, 86, 87, 89
  and social structures 21
self-confidence 46, 61 see also confidence
self-consciousness 57, 58, 85–6

self-control 21, 22
self-discipling 45
self-dishonesty 81
self-doubt 46, 63
self-esteem, low 47, 63
self-fulfilment 35
self-help 68, 70, 71, 72, 80
self-hood, definition of 60
self-improvement therapeutic cultures 61
self-monitoring 45, 62, 65
self-reflection, increased 31
self-regulation 23, 43, 46
self-reproach 34
self-responsibility 30, 31
self-restraint 22
self-revelation 80
self-scrutiny 35
self-surveillance 43, 44
self-transformation 45, 64
self-validation 35, 63
sensation 35
sensations 28, 83
sensibility 44, 45–6, 83
sentiments, expression of 88
Serotonin 85
service workers, emotional management of 14, 23
sex and sexuality 79, 83, 86, 88, 89, 90
*Sex and the City* (Bushnell) 84
sexual coercion and violence 90–1
sexual democracy 81
sexual fields 88
sexual love and relations 22, 83, 86, 88, 89
sexual politics 49
shame 8, 12, 14, 32, 42, 67, 73–4
single-person dwellings, increase in number of 71–2
skills training 89
sociability 87, 90
social abjection 76–7
  and social justice 8
social action and actors 47, 86
social and cultural tensions 86
social behaviour 13
social bonds, short-term 36
social capital 54
social change 26, 27–8, 49, 50
social class and emotions 14, 33, 54–6, 66
social constructionism 22, 23, 40, 51
social difference 64
social drift 71
social etiquette 16, 30
social inclusion and gratification 36
social indicators 69
social interactions, history of 15, 16
social life 68–9
social media platforms 36 see also media industries and advertising
social mobility 87

social movements 70–1
social networks 91
social norms 18, 23, 38, 56, 72
social relationships 57, 87
social solidarity 13, 54
social structure 12, 15–16, 23, 33, 34, 40, 48, 70
  *see also* marriage; parents and parenting
social-structural conditions 34 *see also* age and age limitation; gender
social theory and theorizing 1–2, 22–6
social value 88
social well-being 69
societal progress 69
society
  differentiation of 21
  and individualization in late modernity 26, 71–2, 80–1
  obligations to 80
  post-industrial 30–1
  postmodern 85–6
socio-demographic factors 33 *see also* age and age limitation; education; family and home; race
socio-historical research 73–4, 78–80, 82, 83
sociology of emotions 13, 76, 82, 87
Southeast Asia, intimacy in 91–2
state
  individuals and 82, 92
  withdrawal of from social provision 44
status and wealth 11, 14, 72, 78, 85, 86, 92
status shields 33
stereotypes 90
stranger 67
stratification 14
structural conditions and effects 27, 65
structural functionalism 25
structural inequalities 44, 46, 64
style identity 64
subject 13, 41, 43, 57, 63, 65, 73, 89–90
subjectification 44
subjective–objective distinctions 16–17
subjectivities 60, 61, 89, 90
subjectivity and sociality 26, 45, 46, 90
sub-systems, functional 21
suffering 13, 74–5, 87
suicide rates 48
survival of species 85
symbol 39, 57
symbolic form, inversion of 84
symbolic interactionism 22, 23, 54
systems theory 125

**T**

taboos 81
target users 64
technology 31, 36
  of self 46, 60, 61 *see also* confidence
terrorist attacks 75

Testosterone 85
theorizing agency 61
therapeutic culture and model 30, 32, 61, 70, 72, 80
therapeutic turn 68
therapy and therapists 30, 42, 86
threat 75
toxic insecurity 46
toxic states 47, 63 *see also* self-doubt
traditional authorities 30, 31
traditional feminist discourse 46
traditional gender roles, emancipation of women from 36
traditional housewives 72
traditional societies, alleged emotionality of 20
traditions, decline of 81
tranquillity 34
transcendence 84
transformation and change 26, 43, 64, 65–6, 71, 88, 89
transsexuals, male-to-female 33
trauma, individual and collective 8
*Tumblr* 46

**U**

ugly feelings 42, 76 *see also* disgust; hatred and dislike
uncertainties 29
unconscious 27, 85
under-benefiting and over-benefiting 34
underreporting of mental health issues 48
understanding, social and political framework of 8
underwear and outerware, historical development of meaning of 156
unhappiness, queer 72
upgrading 35
US Black Career Women's Network 61
utilitarian movement 68
utopian and dystopian language 70–1

**V**

values 42, 82, 88
Vasopressin 85
Victorian sexual repression and waiting 79, 83
vocabularies 44–5, 66
vulnerabilities 46, 48, 80, 87

**W**

waiting 83
warmth 81
ways of being and living 60, 71
wealth and status 11, 14, 72, 78, 85, 86, 92
well-being 68, 69, 82
Western
  developed societies 30
  origins of romantic love 78, 79

White men, ethnographic studies into 49, 50, 92
whiteness, boundaries around 46
widowhood 22
women
  African-American 61
  Asian 91–2
  Black 63, 61
  and capital 54
  of colour 46, 64
  contradictory pressures placed on 92–3
  control of romantic encounters by 88
  emancipation of 36
  emotional lives and labour of 33–4, 41
  expectations of 90, 92–3
  exploitation of bodies of 45, 89
  feelings of inferiority and lack of self-worth of 63
  generation of ideas of pure relationship and confluent love by 80
  in heterosexual relationships 46, 84, 88–9, 91, 92–3
  instruction of in how to appeal to and please men 89
  internalization of responsibility by 62
  lower middle-class 56
  middle-class 61, 65–6
  mixed-heritage 63
  need, ambition and confidence 62
  need, psychological intervention 61
  personal experiences of schooling 55
  positioning of 46
  professional 61
  re-cycling of male feeling rules to 81
  regulatory framework for 45
  requirements for change 62
  responsibility of for maintaining relationships 54
  sexual access to and agency of 51, 91
  surveillance of 45
  upper class 56
  White 61, 63, 65–6
  and work 62
  working-class 55, 56
  young, single, well-educated 91–3
women's bodies 51, 64
women's psyches, changing and makeover of 62, 64
women's rights 45 *see also* feminism
work, anger within 10–11
workers, resorting of to feeling rules 60
workforce, emotionalization of 58
working class 55, 56, 78
workplace 16, 56, 61
worth, social sense of 35, 63, 87
wretchedness 8, 67

## Z

zeitgeist, new 61